BrightRED Revision

Higher MATHS

MC Davis

First published in 2008 by:

Bright Red Publishing Ltd
6 Stafford Street
Edinburgh
EH3 7AU

A CIP record for this book is available from the British Library

ISBN 978-1-906736-04-0

With thanks to Ken Vail Graphic Design, Cambridge (layout) and Ivor Normand (copy-edit)

Cover design by Caleb Rutherford – 'Eidetic'

Illustrations by Phillip Burrows and Ken Vail Graphic Design, Cambridge.

Acknowledgements

Every effort has been made to seek all copyright holders. If any have been overlooked then Bright Red Publishing will be delighted to make the necessary arrangements.

CONTENTS

SYLLABUS AND ASSESSMENT

INTRODUCTION

Congratulations on achieving the level necessary to study for Higher Mathematics! The Higher course is intended to take one year from Credit or Intermediate 2 level, assuming you work steadily .

This book is to help you revise for your Higher Mathematics exam. It's going to be of most use to you once you have covered most of the first two units and are preparing for your prelim exam – that's probably from January through to the exam in May. Topics in Unit 3, which are unlikely to be covered before January, have been indicated in the headings so that you know to omit them if you use this book to prepare for your prelim exam.

This book puts the topics of Higher into chapters by their main theme rather than where they come in the course. For example, all the differentiation and integration from the three Units is brought together into one Calculus chapter. This should help you get more of a picture of the topics as a whole as you pull everything together for the final exam.

This book revisits the course for those who have been learning it systematically already. It is not detailed enough to use to learn from scratch – for that, you need a teacher and a textbook. This book is not a substitute for your textbook – which will have far more detail and opportunities for practice, and is still less a substitute for attending classes! If you have to miss a lesson, catch up as soon as you possibly can.

THE EXAM

You must pass all three Unit tests and the final exam in May. The Unit tests contain very specific types of question at level C pass standard only – and you can resit them. Your school or centre will guide you here. However, there is a lot more to passing the final exam. Do not think that, just because you're passing the Unit tests easily, you will necessarily be fine for the final exam.

A few parts of the course are designated A/B level. Some sections and examples in this book are indicated as A/B. In the exam A/B questions are likely to be towards the end of the paper, or at the end of a long question. It does not follow that knowing A/B material will get you an A or a B but it is unlikely that you will without knowing them. A/B topics should be the first things to leave out if you feel you can't cope with everything or are only aiming for a C pass this year.

HOW TO USE THIS BOOK

It's best to do small chunks of revision regularly. If you get tired and confused, take a short break, and then come back to it later.

The Contents list should help you find sections of work you want to target and there is also an index at the end of the book.

If you are fairly confident, try to work out each example for yourself before reading through the working and explanation. It's easy to think you can do something just because you can follow someone else's working. Using this book together with past exam questions is a good way to make progress: review a topic, then practise questions on that topic.

Each double-page spread contains a 'Let's think about this' section which takes different forms. Some have questions designed to test your knowledge and understanding of the content. Others are designed to extend your knowledge of the subject and provide additional interest. Answers are also provided, either immediately after the questions or on pages 92–93.

contd

How to use this book   contd

Ask your teacher for more advice if you get stuck – your teacher will be pleased to see that you are serious about independent study. If your school offers homework clubs or after-school study, or if you have a tutor, keep a note of problems you had in your personal study and take the list in with you for expert help focused on your individual needs.

CALCULATOR

In Paper 1, you are not allowed to use a calculator. In Paper 2, you must have at least a scientific calculator. It is fine to use one of the more advanced calculators such as one with the facility to draw graphs. The exam-setters are expert in setting questions which will be fair for all. If you are in any doubt about your calculator's suitability, check it out with your teacher.

ALGEBRA AND CALCULATION SKILLS

It is important that you are competent working with algebra – powers, fractions, indices and so on – without a calculator. Many candidates gain a Credit pass in Standard Grade with less than full competence here. It is important to build up these skills, preferably early on in Higher, as all mistakes are taken seriously in the Higher exam and lose you marks. Carelessness with copying, making mistakes because you misread your own writing – these will lose you marks. Become a careful, methodical worker!

WEBSITES

The website of the Scottish Qualifications Authority is good to know about. You can find Past Exam questions there. You can also find the full contents list for the course. A/B level material is indicated in the list. However, ploughing through it is fairly tough going; your course notes from your teacher will be more user-friendly. On the SQA website, you should choose "Services for learners", then select Mathematics from the drop-down menu.

www.hsn.net has excellent course notes and worked examples. The BBC Bitesize website has a section on Higher Maths – www.bbc.co.uk/scotland/bitesize. The Scholar website (Heriot-Watt University) is also excellent – if your school has arranged a user name for you, then you will find plenty on which to practise there.

If you are skilled at 'Googling', you can find interesting and stimulating sites on many maths topics, some written for your level. Be cautious on English and American websites, as the content of courses will not be identical, so for your revision make sure you stick to material you know is in your course. This could provide an interesting (short!) break from book-based revision.

The SQA website has useful information on the exam at www.sqa.org.uk

Finally, remember that the rewards of a pass in Higher Mathematics are well worth it! It is certainly not everyone who can do maths at this level, and your pass will surely help you get the future you want for yourself. Good luck, and ENJOY!

COORDINATE GEOMETRY OF THE STRAIGHT LINE

"The straight line" is usually the first part of the Higher course that you will study. Usually, the exam questions on it are done well. It's a great source of straightforward marks in the exam, often right at the start of the paper. Revising it later in the course helps you with the bits you may not have fully understood the first time round.

GRADIENT OF THE STRAIGHT LINE

GRADIENT: $m = \tan \theta$

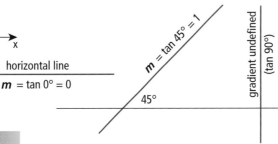

The gradient of a straight line is **the tangent of the angle the line makes with the positive direction of the x-axis**. Any convenient section of the line can be taken to find lengths of the opposite and adjacent sides, and the ratio $\tan \theta = \frac{opp}{adj}$ calculated.

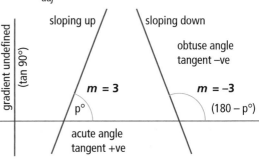

DON'T FORGET

Gradients and angles don't look the correct size in a coordinate diagram unless you have the same scales on both axes.

As the slope becomes steeper, the gradient increases.

At 45°, the gradient is 1 ($\tan 45° = 1$).

Over 45°, the gradient increases rapidly.

Vertical lines: $m = \tan 90°$, which is undefined (there is no numerical value that can be calculated for it).

Parallel lines have the same gradient.

Here is an example to show you how gradients and tangent can link up in a question.

OPQR is a kite. Find the gradient of OP correct to 2 dp.

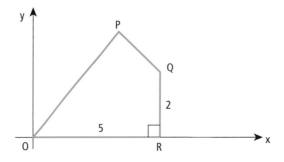

DON'T FORGET

Don't confuse $\frac{0}{a} = 0$ with $\frac{a}{0}$, which is undefined.

OQ is the line of symmetry of the kite.

$\tan Q\hat{O}R = \frac{2}{5}$

$Q\hat{O}R = \tan^{-1} 0\cdot4 = 21\cdot8°$

Hence POR = $43\cdot6°$

$m_{OP} = \tan P\hat{O}R = \mathbf{0\cdot95}$

GRADIENT FORMULA USING COORDINATES

The formula is $m = \dfrac{y_2 - y_1}{x_2 - x_1}$ (provided $x_1 \neq x_2$) "change in y divided by change in x", or "vertical change over horizontal change". We are calculating the same ratio as "opposite over adjacent" in the tangent ratio.

Suppose, in the first diagram on the opposite page, A is the point (–1, 1) and B is (5, 4).

Substituting gives $m_{AB} = \dfrac{4-1}{5-(-1)} = \dfrac{3}{6} = \dfrac{1}{2}$

It doesn't matter which order you take the points in, so long as you are consistent on the top and bottom of the fraction.

(Mistakes happen if you don't subtract negatives correctly, or if you mix up x and y.)

The angle θ in the first diagram can now be calculated: $\theta = \tan^{-1} 0\cdot5 = 26\cdot6°$.

PERPENDICULAR LINES

If two lines are perpendicular, then $m_1 \times m_2 = -1$. This is used in two main ways.

First,

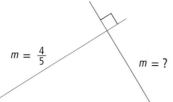

$m = \dfrac{4}{5}$ $m = ?$

m_2 will be the negative reciprocal of m_1. Invert the fraction and change its sign: $-\dfrac{5}{4}$

Second,

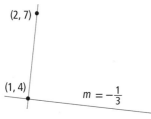

(2, 7)

(1, 4) $m = -\dfrac{1}{3}$

To show that the lines are perpendicular,

work out the second gradient: $m = \dfrac{7-4}{2-1} = 3$

so $m_1 \times m_2 = 3 \times -\dfrac{1}{3} = -1$.

That's good, but remember also to tell the exam-marker **why** this shows that the lines are perpendicular. "Since $m_1 \times m_2 = -1$, the lines are perpendicular" needs to be written down in your answer.

COLLINEARITY

Given that the gradients of PQ and PR are the same,

R

Q

P

can you place these points in any way other than in one straight line? No – it's impossible. The three points are collinear – they lie on the same straight line.

LET'S THINK ABOUT THIS

What other topic in the course is useful for proving collinearity?

EQUATION OF THE STRAIGHT LINE

$y - b = m(x - a)$

To use this equation, you need to know the gradient, **m**, and the coordinates of a point on the line (**a**, **b**). You can use it given just two points by finding the gradient first.

Example 1

Find the equation of the line through $(\frac{1}{3}, -\frac{5}{6})$ with gradient $-\frac{1}{2}$

Substituting: $y - (-\frac{5}{6}) = -\frac{1}{2}(x - \frac{1}{3})$. That's it done, but it doesn't look very tidy.

So, continuing to simplify (and it's a nasty one with fractions and negatives, so care is needed):

first sort out the double negative and multiply through by 6 to remove denominators.

$6y + 5 = -3(x - \frac{1}{3})$ (remember not to multiply what's **inside** the brackets)

Next, multiply out the bracket: $6y + 5 = -3x + 1$
Then collect like terms: $6y = -3x - 4$

It's now looking very acceptable.

How far should you simplify it? Don't agonise too much – there are often clues.

1   If it's in the multiple-choice section, just simplify it until you can tell which option it matches.

2   It could be part (a) of a longer question with a part (b), and you can't do (b) without simplifying it.

> ### DON'T FORGET
>
> Sometimes, you could be unsure whether to simplify an answer in part (a). Quite often, you need the result in part (b) anyway. In such a case, it won't matter where in the question you simplify it – the exam-marker will find it wherever it is and give you the marks.

$Ax + By + C = 0$

Lines are sometimes written this way (with A, B and C integers – no fractions) as it looks neat and consistent. It's a good way to write equations if you are going to solve them simultaneously, as it means the terms are nicely lined up ready to go. The line $6y = -3x - 4$ above would rearrange to give $3x + 6y + 4 = 0$.

If A = 0 we have lines like $y = 3$, $y = -4$, $y = \frac{1}{2}$ ... vertical lines.

If B = 0 we have lines like $x = 1$, $x = 39$, $x = -2$ ... horizontal lines.

Don't mix them up!

> ### DON'T FORGET
>
> The **x-axis** is horizontal and has equation **y = 0**, and the **y-axis** is vertical and has equation **x = 0**.

$y = mx + c$

c is the intercept on the y-axis, and as usual **m** stands for the gradient.

Our line from the example above can easily be put into this form by dividing through by 6:
$y = -\frac{1}{2}x - \frac{2}{3}$

It is the form which gives us the best picture of what the line looks like on the page. The line has gradient $-\frac{1}{2}$ and cuts the y-axis at $(0, -\frac{2}{3})$.

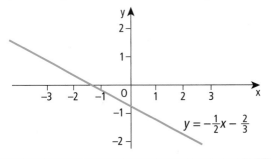

contd

$y = mx + c$ contd

Example 2

Does (4, 3) lie on the line $y = 2x - 3$?

Substituting the coordinates to see if they satisfy the equation: $3 = 2 \times 4 - 3$ leads to $3 = 5$ which is clearly not true, so the point does not lie on the line.

Example 3

$(a, -13)$ lies on the line $y = 2x + 3$. Find a.

Substituting: $-13 = 2a + 3$
$$2a = -16$$
$$a = -8$$

> **DON'T FORGET**
>
> A point lies on a line, or a circle, if its coordinates satisfy the equation when substituted.

MIDPOINT OF A LINE

In simple examples, especially if the coordinates are positive, this can be done by inspection –

$x_M = 5$, since 5 is midway between 2 and 8. A bit more care is needed for the y-coordinate. Using the midpoint formula can be safer, especially where negatives are involved:

$$M\left(\frac{x_1 + x_2}{2}, \frac{y_1 + y_2}{2}\right) = \left(\frac{2 + 8}{2}, \frac{7 + (-5)}{2}\right)$$

So, M is the point (5, 1).

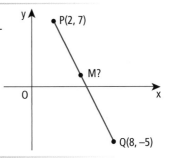

DISTANCE FORMULA

$$d = \sqrt{(x_2 - x_1)^2 + (y_2 - y_1)^2}$$

The values for the formula can again often be found by inspection – especially with a good sketch. After all, we are just finding the values to use in Pythagoras' Theorem. For the length of PQ, the vertical distance between the points is clearly 12 units, and the horizontal (slightly less easy) is 6 units.

P(2, 7)

$y_P + y_Q$ (12)

d

$$d = \sqrt{12^2 + (-6)^2}$$
$$= \sqrt{180}$$
$$= 13 \cdot 4$$

Q(8, −5)

$x_P - x_Q$ (−6)

> **DON'T FORGET**
>
> Sketches – quick and easy – are a huge help in the Straight Line work. Use a pencil and make the sketch big enough to be helpful. You can use the one in the question paper if you like, but it is better to let the exam-marker see what you are doing.

Example 4

Find the equation of the locus of points equidistant from P and Q. "Locus" just means position (in Latin). Some experimentation plotting a few points satisfying the description shows we have a line perpendicular to PQ and bisecting PQ.

We already have M(5, 1), the midpoint.

Gradient of PQ: $m = \frac{-5 - 7}{8 - 2} = -\frac{12}{6} = -2$

The gradient of the perpendicular to PQ will be $\frac{1}{2}$ since $-2 \times \frac{1}{2} = -1$

The equation of the line $y - 1 = \frac{1}{2}(x - 5)$
$$2y - 2 = x - 5$$
$$2y = x - 3$$

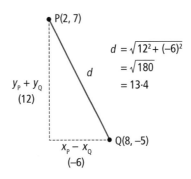

possible positions for the points lie on the perpendicular bisector of PQ

LET'S THINK ABOUT THIS

In finding the midpoint of a line, we are using basically the same maths as the Section Formula from the Vectors topic. Try finding N, the point which is two thirds of the way from P to Q in Example 4.

GEOMETRY PROBLEMS USING THE STRAIGHT LINE

LINES IN QUADRILATERALS

Most problems require you to use the geometric properties of the shapes, so you must be familiar with them.

Squares, rectangles, parallelograms and rhombuses have opposite sides equal (**distance formula**) and parallel (**equal gradients**). They all have diagonals which bisect each other, so the **midpoint formula** could be handy. Squares and rectangles have sides meeting at right angles, and the diagonals of squares, kites and rhombuses are perpendicular, so $m_1 \times m_2 = -1$ could be important.

Example 5

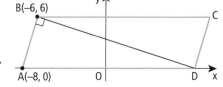

ABCD is a parallelogram. AB is perpendicular to BD.
a Find the equation of BD.
b Find P, the point of intersection of the diagonals.
c Find the coordinates of C.

a For line BD, we know a point (B) and can use gradient of AB to find gradient of BD:

$$m_{AB} = \frac{6-0}{-6+8} = \frac{6}{2} = 3$$
$$\text{So } m_{BD} = -\frac{1}{3}$$
$$\text{Equation: } y - 6 = -\frac{1}{3}(x + 6)$$
$$3y - 18 = -x - 6$$
$$\mathbf{3y = 12 - x}$$

b The diagonals bisect each other, so the point of intersection will be the midpoint of BD (or AC, but BD is easier to find). D lies on **3y = 12 − x** and $y_D = 0$, so $x_D = 12$ (by substitution into the equation of the line).
The midpoint of BD: B(−6, 6) D(12, 0) so midpoint P is **(3, 3)**

c It's easy to find P in several ways, and you don't need any working written (but remember working is also for **your** benefit – to avoid mistakes being made by carrying too much in your head).
You could use the midpoint formula with P and AC.

Or you could use the fact that BC is horizontal and equal in length to AD (20 units).

Or use vectors $\overrightarrow{DC} = \overrightarrow{AB} = \begin{pmatrix} 2 \\ 6 \end{pmatrix}$ ... result **C(14, 6)**

LINES IN TRIANGLES

You also need to know about the following lines in triangles.

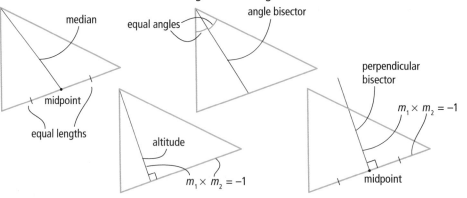

contd

LINES IN TRIANGLES contd

The really interesting thing about each of these sets of lines is that, in any triangle, they are **concurrent** – that is, they all intersect at the same point. In each of the examples above, only one of the special lines has been drawn in. If this is your own book, you could sketch in the other two (lightly, in pencil) in each diagram and see for yourself.

It's not very likely at all that three *random* lines will be concurrent. If they are parallel, they won't even meet. Even when none are parallel, it's more likely they will look like diagram 1 than diagram 2 here:

1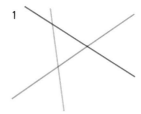

2

Example 6

Are these three lines concurrent? $2x + y - 2 = 0$
$x - y + 5 = 0$
$x - 3y + 13 = 0$

And how to do it? First, find the point of intersection of two of the lines (we can see from the coefficients that none of the lines are parallel, so any two must intersect if you extend them far enough – a diagram should convince you). Then, see whether that point also lies on the third line.

Adding equations 1 and 2 gives: $3x + 3 = 0 \Rightarrow x = -1$
Substitution in equation 1 gives: $-2 + y - 2 = 0 \Rightarrow y = 4$ $(-1, 4)$

Now, test to see whether $(-1, 4)$ satisfies equation 3: $x - 3y + 13 = -1 - 12 + 13 = 0$

Yes it does, so **the three lines are concurrent**, and the point of concurrency is $(-1, 4)$.

Example 7

In the diagram, BM is a median and CP an altitude of triangle ABC. Find the point of intersection of BM and CP.

We need the equations of the two lines. We already know one point on each.

For BM, we find M, the midpoint of AC: $M\left(\frac{-12 + 4}{2}, \frac{3 + 1}{2}\right) = M(-4, 2)$

We can now find the gradient of BM: $m = \frac{-7 - 2}{-7 + 4} = 3$

So, **equation of BM** is $y - 2 = 3(x + 4)$ (using point M)
$y = 3x + 14$

For the gradient of CP, we must first find the gradient of AB: $m = \frac{3 + 7}{-12 + 7} = -2$

So, gradient of CP $= \frac{1}{2}$ (perpendicular to AB, remember).

Equation of CP is $y - 1 = \frac{1}{2}(x - 4)$ (using point C)
$2y = x - 2$

Solving the equations of the two lines simultaneously to find the point of intersection gives $(-6, -4)$, which you can check out for yourself.

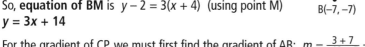

A(–12, 3)   M   y   C(4, 1)   x   P   B(–7, –7)

> **DON'T FORGET**
>
> Straight lines will intersect each other unless they are parallel. It's not at all likely that three straight lines will intersect at the same point (concurrency).

> **DON'T FORGET**
>
> If lines are concurrent, there will be one point which lies on all of them.

LET'S THINK ABOUT THIS

The points of intersection of the medians, altitudes and perpendicular bisectors are normally different points. Where would all three be the same point?

COORDINATE GEOMETRY OF THE CIRCLE

This is another section on geometry in two dimensions. The work of the Straight Line section is used a great deal here also, as many of the questions are about tangents and chords. Circle questions are often quite lengthy, in several parts. Often, an earlier part will be a "Show that ..."-style question, which means if you get stuck you are not prevented from going on to the next part, as the question tells you the "answer" to the first part anyway.

EQUATION OF THE CIRCLE

DIFFERENT FORMS OF THE CIRCLE EQUATION

$(x - a)^2 + (y - b)^2 = r^2$

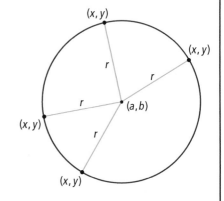

You can see that this is a distance-formula statement telling us that points (x, y) are **a** units away from the point (a, b). The diagram shows a few points plotted which satisfy this condition. We can see that the locus of these points is a circle with centre (a, b) and radius **r** units.

If a circle has a radius 6 and centre $(-2, 5)$, it has equation

$(x + 2)^2 + (y - 5)^2 = 36$

which gives the locus of points (x, y) which are 6 units away from $(-2, 5)$.

Equations are normally presented already multipled out and simplified, which in the case of the circle hides the centre and radius in among the algebra:

Multiplying out the equation above
$$x^2 + 4x + 4 + y^2 - 10y + 25 = 36$$
$$x^2 + y^2 + 4x - 10y - 7 = 0$$

When a circle is given in this form, instead of having to do the algebra in reverse to find the centre and radius, the exam formula list gives you what you need:

Circle $x^2 + y^2 + 2gx + 2fy + c = 0$ has centre $(-g, -f)$ and radius $\sqrt{g^2 + f^2 - c}$, provided $g^2 + f^2 - c > 0$

$x^2 + y^2 = r^2$ is the equation of a circle with centre $(0, 0)$ and radius r.

DON'T FORGET

The circle equations are given in the exam formula list at the beginning of each exam paper.

USING THE EQUATION OF A CIRCLE

DON'T FORGET

Notice that the first circle has no linear x term, so its centre will lie on the x-axis. If there is neither a linear x nor y term, the centre is the origin.

Example 1

Here are the equations of two circles. Find the centre and radius of each from the equations.

$x^2 + y^2 - 6y + 5 = 0$
$x^2 + y^2 + 6x - 4y - 23 = 0$

For the first circle, $g = 0$, $f = -3$ and $c = 5$.

This makes the **centre** $(-g, -f)$ the point **(0, 3)** and the **radius** $\sqrt{0^2 + (-3)^2 - 5} = \sqrt{4} = \mathbf{2}$

The second circle gives a little more work: $g = 3$, $f = -2$, $c = -23$

leading to **centre (-3, 2)** and **radius** $\sqrt{3^2 + (-2)^2 - (-23)} = \sqrt{9 + 4 + 23} = \mathbf{6}$

contd

USING THE EQUATION OF A CIRCLE contd

Example 2

What is the equation of the circle shown in the diagram?

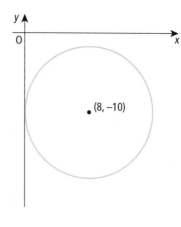

The horizontal line which can be drawn from the centre to the y-axis is a radius of the circle and has length 8. The equation of the circle can easily be obtained by substituting the radius and coordinates of the centre into $(x − a)^2 + (y − b)^2 = r^2$

The equation is $(x − 8)^2 + (y − (−10))^2 = 8^2$
or, more simply, $\mathbf{(x − 8)^2 + (y + 10)^2 = 64}$

> **DON'T FORGET**
>
> There is no need to multiply out brackets and simplify an equation like this unless asked to. It certainly isn't wrong to do so, but no extra marks will be given if you do!

Example 3

Two congruent circles $x^2 + y^2 − 4x − 10y + 4 = 0$
and $\qquad\qquad\qquad x^2 + y^2 + 8x + 6y = 0$
have centres P and Q respectively and touch only at one point, M.

a Find the coordinates of M.
b Find the radius of each circle.

a The circles are positioned as in the diagram, and, being congruent, will have equal radii, so M will be the midpoint of PQ.

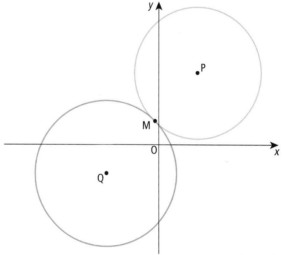

Using $(−g, −f)$ for each circle in turn, we obtain centres P$(2, 5)$ and Q$(−4, −3)$.

Using the midpoint formula, we find $M = \left(\dfrac{2−4}{2}, \dfrac{5−3}{2}\right) = (−1, 1)$ **M(−1, 1)**.

b To find the radius, we have a choice: (1) use the distance formula to find PQ and then find half of it, or (2) find $\sqrt{g^2 + f^2 − c}$ using the values from the equation of either circle.

Using the distance formula, $PQ = \sqrt{(2 + 4)^2 + (5 + 3)^2} = \sqrt{100} = 10$

Hence each circle has **radius 5**.

> **DON'T FORGET**
>
> There are often different correct ways to solve geometry questions. Don't agonise over it – choose whichever one you think will be simplest for you.

Example 4

Does A(−3, 1) lie on, inside or outside the circle with centre P in the example above?

Find the distance of A from P: $AP = \sqrt{5^2 + 4^2} = \sqrt{41} = 6.4$

Since this is more than the radius, which we found was 5, A lies outside the circle.

Alternatively, you can substitute the coordinates of A into the left side of the circle equation: $(−3)^2 + 1^2 − 4 × (−3) − 10 × 1 + 4$ which gives 16, not 0, so point A lies outside the circle.

> **DON'T FORGET**
>
> Warning – don't ever just go by the diagrams, as they are seldom drawn accurately!

LET'S THINK ABOUT THIS

Work out the radius and the coordinates of the centre of the circle with equation
$4x^2 + 4y^2 − 16x + 8y + 11 = 0$

CIRCLES AND TANGENTS

INTERSECTION OF A LINE AND A CIRCLE

Example 5

Find any points of intersection of the line $x = 6$

and the circle $x^2 + y^2 - 4x + 10y + 4 = 0$

To do this, we solve the two equations simultaneously.

Substituting 6 in the place of x in the equation of the circle gives:

$36 + y^2 - 24 + 10y + 4 = 0$

$\Rightarrow y^2 + 10y + 16 = 0$
$\Rightarrow (y + 2)(y + 8) = 0$
$\Rightarrow y = -2, y = -8$

leading to points of intersection
(6, −2) and (6, −8)

A straight line could cut a circle twice, as in this example, or once (a tangent), or not at all.

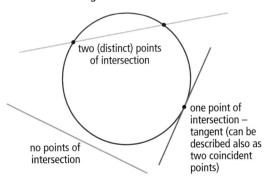

> two (distinct) points of intersection
>
> one point of intersection – tangent (can be described also as two coincident points)
>
> no points of intersection

> **DON'T FORGET**
>
> This is the substitution method for solving equations simultaneously and is a very important skill in Higher Maths.

TANGENTS

When the points of intersection of a circle and a straight line are found, and they are the same, there is one point of intersection (or you could think of it as two coincident points).

A straight line cannot cut a circle once and not be a tangent.

Sometimes you are asked to find whether or not there is tangency, but are not asked to find any actual points of contact. You may then use the fact that the discriminant is zero for tangency, as shown in this next example.

Example 6

Show that the line $y = 3x + 10$ is a tangent to the circle $x^2 + y^2 - 8x - 4y - 20 = 0$

Substitute $3x + 10$ in the place of y in the circle equation, then arrange in standard quadratic form:

$$x^2 + (3x + 10)^2 - 8x - 4(3x + 10) - 20 = 0 \quad \text{... substitution}$$
$$x^2 + 9x^2 + 60x + 100 - 8x - 12x - 40 - 20 = 0 \quad \text{... multiply out}$$
$$10x^2 + 40x + 40 = 0 \quad \text{... simplify}$$
$$x^2 + 4x + 4 = 0$$

At this point, you have a choice: (1) you can go on to solve the equation and you will find two equal solutions, or (2) you can use the fact that, if the discriminant, $b^2 - 4ac$, is zero, then the solutions are equal.

Using the discriminant: $b^2 - 4ac = 4^2 - 4 \times 1 \times 4 = 0$ (show the calculation).

Hence **there are equal roots, so the line is a tangent to the circle**.

The discriminant is dealt with in more detail in the section on the quadratic function.

> **DON'T FORGET**
>
> A straight line stretches to infinity in both directions, even if we only see part of it on the page.

> **DON'T FORGET**
>
> When proving that a line is a tangent, you must state your reason (e.g. only one point of contact), and back it up with the working (your solution for the quadratic equation, or the calculation of the discriminant).

contd

TANGENTS contd

Example 7

The line $x = y - k$ $(k > 0)$ is a tangent to the circle with equation $x^2 + y^2 = 2$

Find the value of k and use it to establish the point of contact.

Substituting into the circle equation: $(y - k)^2 + y^2 = 2$

Expand and simplify:
$$y^2 - 2ky + k^2 + y^2 = 2$$
$$2y^2 - 2ky + k^2 - 2 = 0$$

We now have a quadratic in y, with coefficients $a = 2$, $b = -2k$, $c = k^2 - 2$

For tangency, the discriminant = 0, so put $b^2 - 4ac = 0$

$b^2 - 4ac = 4k^2 - 4 \times 2 \times (k^2 - 2) = 0$
$4k^2 - 8k^2 + 16 = 0$
$4k^2 = 16$
$k = 2$ (disregard –2, as k > 0)

Substituting for k in the working above:
$$2y^2 - 4y + 2 = 0$$
$$y^2 - 2y + 1 = 0$$
$$(y - 1)^2 = 0$$
$$y = 1$$

giving the point of contact **(–1, 1)**.

Example 8

A line with equation $4x + 3y - 43 = 0$ is a tangent to a circle with centre (3, 2).
Find the point of contact.

Because the tangent and radius are perpendicular, the product of their gradients is –1. Draw a rough sketch.

$4x + 3y - 43 = 0$

(3, 2)

Rearrange the tangent equation to find its gradient:

$3y = -4x + 43$

$y = -\frac{4}{3}x + \frac{43}{3}$

So, the gradient of the tangent is $-\frac{4}{3}$ and the gradient of the radius is $\frac{3}{4}$ (since $-\frac{4}{3} \times \frac{3}{4} = -1$).

The equation of the radius can be found using the gradient and the point (3, 2), giving $y - 2 = \frac{3}{4}(x - 3)$
so that $4y = 3x - 1$.

Solving the equations of the radius and the tangent simultaneously gives the point of contact:
(7, 5) ... do the working for yourself.

> **DON'T FORGET**
>
> This example requires the use of the discriminant to find the equation of a tangent. This type of question can be a minefield for those whose algebra is dodgy. Be very careful!

> **DON'T FORGET**
>
> A tangent is perpendicular to the radius at the point of contact.

LET'S THINK ABOUT THIS

Try finding the equation of the **common tangent** in example 3 of this section (see page 13) by solving the equations of the two circles simultaneously.

CIRCLES, CHORDS AND SYMMETRY

CIRCLES AND SYMMETRY

Here are diagrams showing various ways in which circles could be placed in relation to each other.

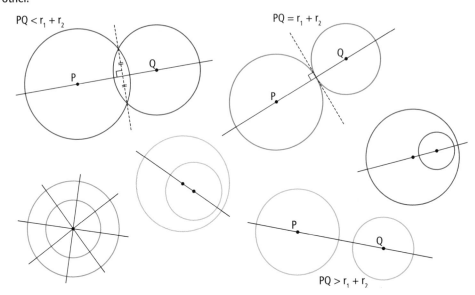

You should notice that the line of centres is a line of symmetry for each pair of circles.

To decide whether the circles intersect at two points, one point or not at all, add the lengths of the two radii together and compare the result with the distance between the centres.

If we use r_1 and r_2 to be the lengths of the radii ($r_1 \geq r_2$), then the circles intersect if $r_1 - r_2 \leq$ distance between centres $\leq r_1 + r_2$.

If you look at the pictures, you can see that this makes sense.

DON'T FORGET

You will do all your Higher exam on blank paper. Draw sketches – they often guide you to the correct method. However, a solution from a scale drawing never gets marks in Higher – you must demonstrate the results by calculation.

In example 1 on page 12, we found the centres and radii of two circles from their equations. Just looking back at the algebra doesn't give us much idea about how the circles look on the page. But, if you drew a **rough sketch**, now that the centres and radii are known, you would probably notice that the second circle looks like it **might** lie completely inside the first.

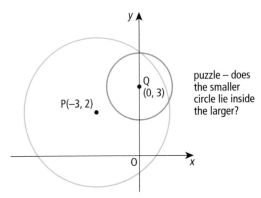

puzzle – does the smaller circle lie inside the larger?

To find out, we must do some calculations. The sketch helps decide what calculation to do – is the distance between the centres (length of PQ) added to the radius of the smaller circle less than the radius of the larger circle? If so, the smaller circle is inside the larger.

Use the distance formula to find the length PQ:

$$PQ = \sqrt{(0 + 3)^2 + (3 - 2)^2} = \sqrt{10} = 3 \cdot 2$$

The distance from P to the further edge of the smaller circle is therefore $2 + 3 \cdot 2 = 5 \cdot 2$

However, the radius of the larger circle is 6, so the smaller circle does indeed lie inside the larger, as we suspected.

COMMON TANGENTS AND THE CIRCLE

Many problems on circles have a problem-solving aspect to them. Before you can show off your knowledge of the algebra techniques to prove tangency or construct the equation of a circle, you must work out just what algebra is relevant to the problem, as in the next example.

Example 9

The circle with centre P has equation $x^2 + y^2 + 2x + 12y + 32 = 0$. The centre, Q, of the other circle in the diagram is the point (1, 5).

The line AB is a common tangent. The point of contact with circle centre P is A(1, –5).

Find

a the equation of the common tangent, AB.
b the equation of the circle with centre Q.

What do we know about circles that could help here? Tangent perpendicular to radius at A and B is vital to solving this problem. Notice that the right angles lead to the two radii in the diagram, AP and BQ, being parallel – important for part (b).

Not all the steps in the working are here – fill in the gaps yourself as you go.

a Already knowing a point (A) on the tangent, we now need its gradient.
From the equation of circle centre P, we know that its centre $(-g, -f)$ will be (–1, –6).

Using the gradient formula leads to
$m_{AP} = \frac{1}{2}$
$m_{AB} = -2$

Substituting this gradient and coordinates of A into $y = mx + c$, the equation of the tangent is: $y = -2x - 3$

b Knowing Q, the centre of the other circle, we now need the length of the radius in order to construct the equation of the circle centre Q. What do we know?

The gradients of AP and BQ are equal, so $m_{BQ} = \frac{1}{2}$

The equation of BQ is $y - 5 = \frac{1}{2}(x - 1)$
$2y = x + 9$

B is the point of intersection of the lines BQ and AB, so solve the equations of these lines simultaneously: AB $y = -2x - 3$
and   BQ $2y = x + 9$ to find B.

Multiply the second equation by 2 and add: $5y - 15 = 0$
$y = 3$

Substitute to find x: $x = -3$ B is the point (–3, 3)

Using the distance formula with points B and Q, the radius of the circle is
$\sqrt{(-3 - 1)^2 + (3 - 5)^2} = \sqrt{20}$

Using the circle formula, the equation of the circle, centre Q(1, 5):
$(x - 1)^2 + (y - 5)^2 = 20$

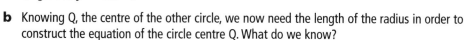

y

• Q(1, 5)

B

O x

A(1, –5)

P•

⚙ LET'S THINK ABOUT THIS

Not every equation which **looks** like it represents a circle actually does represent a circle.
For example, $x^2 + y^2 + 2x - 6y + 50 = 0$ **isn't** the equation of a circle. Why not?

COORDINATE GEOMETRY OF VECTORS

Vectors are used in physics and mechanics to deal with forces such as gravity, velocity and weight.

A large part of the vectors work in Higher Maths is the study of vectors represented by directed lines in three-dimensional space, with the axes at right angles to each other. This makes it a very useful topic for solving problems on shapes in three dimensions.

The results also hold in two dimensions, and the calculations would be just the same but without z-coordinates and z-components – but you can expect the questions in the exam to be about three dimensions. Generally, problems in two dimensions are dealt with by the geometry in the Straight Line section.

Vectors questions are usually done well in the Higher exam. Know the topic well and you will have a whole bunch of marks you can be sure of getting fairly quickly and easily.

COORDINATES AND COMPONENTS

WORKING WITH COORDINATES AND COMPONENTS

E (5, 3, 4) is a point in three-dimensional space (see diagram below). $\mathbf{e} = \begin{pmatrix} 5 \\ 3 \\ 4 \end{pmatrix}$ is a vector and must be written with the components vertical.

In the diagram below, the position vector $\mathbf{e}$ is the directed line segment OE, and gives the components of the move from O, the origin, to E. $\mathbf{e}$ is the *position vector* of E because it fixes its position. There can only be one point E. However, there can be any number of representations of the vector $\mathbf{e}$ because every vector with the same components is an identical move or journey, but starting in a different place in space.

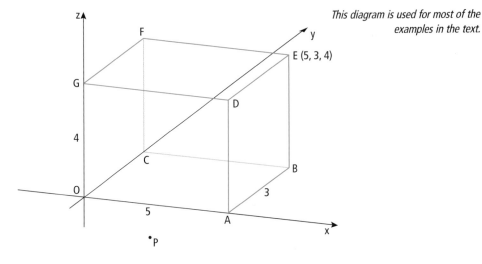

This diagram is used for most of the examples in the text.

The cuboid pictured has been drawn on a coordinate diagram with x, y and z-axes in three dimensions at right angles to each other. Point P lies under the cuboid.

E is the point (5, 3, 4), so OA = 5 units, OC = 3 units and OG = 4 units in length.

Important and very useful result: $\vec{AB} = \mathbf{b} - \mathbf{a}$, which it's very easy to verify for particular cases of vectors and points on coordinate diagrams.

contd

WORKING WITH COORDINATES AND COMPONENTS contd

Example 1

$\overrightarrow{PF} = \begin{pmatrix} -3 \\ 1 \\ 10 \end{pmatrix}$ Find the coordinates of P.

F (0, 3, 4) is easily deduced from the diagram.

Since $\overrightarrow{PF} = \mathbf{f} - \mathbf{p}$, substitution gives us $\begin{pmatrix} -3 \\ 1 \\ 10 \end{pmatrix} = \begin{pmatrix} 0 \\ 3 \\ 4 \end{pmatrix} - \mathbf{p}$

This vector equation is easily rearranged and solved to give

$\mathbf{p} = \begin{pmatrix} 3 \\ 2 \\ -6 \end{pmatrix}$ so **P is the point (3, 2, –6)**.

USING VECTOR PATHWAYS

This is basic to understanding vectors. A simple case is $\overrightarrow{AB} = \mathbf{b} - \mathbf{a}$ above.

The vector sum $\overrightarrow{FE} + \overrightarrow{PF} - \overrightarrow{PE}$ can be rearranged

$= \overrightarrow{FE} + \overrightarrow{PF} + \overrightarrow{EP}$ ($\overrightarrow{EP}$ is the negative of $\overrightarrow{PE}$ – same magnitude, opposite direction)

$= \overrightarrow{FE} + \overrightarrow{EP} + \overrightarrow{PF}$ (vectors can be added in any order).

This gives a continuous route from F back to F – resulting in no change of position at all!

We have the components of $\overrightarrow{PF}$ above, and it is easy to work out the components of $\overrightarrow{FE}$ and $\overrightarrow{EP}$.

Using components, $\overrightarrow{FE} + \overrightarrow{EP} + \overrightarrow{PF} = \begin{pmatrix} 5 \\ 0 \\ 0 \end{pmatrix} + \begin{pmatrix} -2 \\ -1 \\ -10 \end{pmatrix} + \begin{pmatrix} -3 \\ 1 \\ 10 \end{pmatrix} = \begin{pmatrix} 0 \\ 0 \\ 0 \end{pmatrix}$

The result is the zero vector – unsurprising, as we finished where we started.

Another illustration of vector paths is the result for finding the midpoint of a line. If M is the midpoint of $\overrightarrow{EP}$, then the diagram here shows

$\mathbf{m} = \frac{1}{2}(\mathbf{a} + \mathbf{b})$

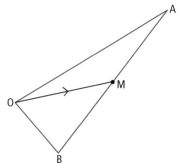

$\mathbf{m} = \overrightarrow{OM} \quad = \overrightarrow{OA} + \frac{1}{2}\overrightarrow{AB}$ start at O, move to A, then halfway along $\overrightarrow{AB}$

$= \mathbf{a} + \frac{1}{2}(\mathbf{b} - \mathbf{a})$

$= \frac{1}{2}\mathbf{a} + \frac{1}{2}\mathbf{b}$

$= \frac{1}{2}(\mathbf{a} + \mathbf{b})$

> **DON'T FORGET**
>
> Make sure you get the signs of the components correct when you are taking them from a coordinate diagram. It's all too easy to reverse them!

> **DON'T FORGET**
>
> Remember $\frac{1}{2}\mathbf{a}$ is **a** with all components halved.

LET'S THINK ABOUT THIS

Although we introduce O to do the working, notice that the result doesn't depend on where O is but only on the positions of A and B in relation to each other.

Establish the result $\overrightarrow{AB} = \mathbf{b} - \mathbf{a}$, again by introducing O.

MAGNITUDE, COLLINEARITY AND THE SECTION FORMULA

MAGNITUDE OF A VECTOR AND THE DISTANCE FORMULA

DON'T FORGET

Don't go on to give an approximate answer by evaluating the square root, unless it is clear from the question that this is wanted, or is helpful for what you have to do next.

Example 2

Find $|\vec{PF}|$, the magnitude or length of $\vec{PF}$.

Magnitude is calculated using Pythagoras' Theorem, extended to three dimensions:

$$|\vec{PF}| = \sqrt{(-3)^2 + 1^2 + 10^2)} = \sqrt{110}$$

In general, the distance between two points (x_1, y_1, z_1) and (x_2, y_2, z_2) is

$$d = \sqrt{(x_2 - x_1)^2 + (y_2 - y_1)^2 + (z_2 - z_1)^2}$$

which you will recognise as the distance formula, again extended to three dimensions. If you substitute the coordinates of P and F, you will find you are soon working out exactly the same as in the first calculation above.

UNIT VECTORS

These have length 1. Examples are **i**, **j** and **k**, which take the directions of the three axes

$$\mathbf{i} = \begin{pmatrix} 1 \\ 0 \\ 0 \end{pmatrix} \quad \mathbf{j} = \begin{pmatrix} 0 \\ 1 \\ 0 \end{pmatrix} \quad \mathbf{k} = \begin{pmatrix} 0 \\ 0 \\ 1 \end{pmatrix} \quad \text{so that} \quad \mathbf{e} = \begin{pmatrix} 5 \\ 3 \\ 4 \end{pmatrix} = 5\mathbf{i} + 3\mathbf{j} + 4\mathbf{k}$$

Example 3

Find a unit vector, **u**, parallel to $\vec{PF}$.

u will be a scalar multiple of $\vec{PF}$ (in order to be parallel).
$\vec{PF}$ has length $\sqrt{110}$ and **u** has length 1. Dividing each component of $\vec{PF}$ by $\sqrt{110}$ will make its length 1.

$$\mathbf{u} = \frac{1}{\sqrt{110}} \begin{pmatrix} 3 \\ 2 \\ -6 \end{pmatrix} \quad \text{or} \quad \mathbf{u} = \frac{-1}{\sqrt{110}} \begin{pmatrix} 3 \\ 2 \\ -6 \end{pmatrix} \quad \text{(no need to evaluate further unless the question requires it).}$$

COLLINEAR POINTS AND THE SECTION FORMULA

DON'T FORGET

parallel lines + common point = collinearity.

DON'T FORGET

That there is a common point must be stated to avoid losing marks!

If you found that two lines had the same gradient, you would know they were parallel. If you also knew that a particular point lay on both lines, then the two lines would no longer be separate lines but would both be parts of the same straight line.

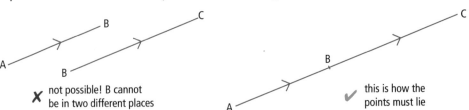

✗ not possible! B cannot be in two different places

✓ this is how the points must lie

The vector work in this section does the same thing, but can be used in three dimensions (as well as two, should you want to). To show that lines are parallel using vectors, show that one is a scalar multiple of the other (as shown below). If the lines/vectors also have a point in common, then they are one line and all the points lie on the same line, i.e. are collinear.

contd

COLLINEAR POINTS AND THE SECTION FORMULA contd

Example 4

Show that A(3, –1, 5), B(6, 0, 3) and C(15, 3, –3) are collinear points, and draw a diagram to show their relative positions.

Choose any two directed line segments using these points.

Choosing $\overrightarrow{AB}$ and $\overrightarrow{AC}$:

$$\overrightarrow{AB} = \begin{pmatrix} 6-3 \\ 0+1 \\ 3-5 \end{pmatrix} = \begin{pmatrix} 3 \\ 1 \\ -2 \end{pmatrix} \text{ and } \overrightarrow{AC} = \begin{pmatrix} 15-3 \\ 3+1 \\ -3-5 \end{pmatrix} = \begin{pmatrix} 12 \\ 4 \\ -8 \end{pmatrix} = 4\begin{pmatrix} 3 \\ 1 \\ -2 \end{pmatrix}$$

$\overrightarrow{AC} = 4\overrightarrow{AB}$ (i.e. $\overrightarrow{AC}$ is a scalar multiple of $\overrightarrow{AB}$) is easily spotted once the components are calculated; and, since A is a common point, A, B and C are collinear points.

Next, draw a line – the direction is irrelevant – and mark the points A, B and C on it so that AC is four times the length of AB.

> **DON'T FORGET**
>
> Notice that
> AB:BC = 1:3
> while AB:AC = 1:4.
> Diagrams like this will help you not to make mistakes based on exactly which line segments are which. It's wise to draw a sketch in these situations whether or not you are asked to.

Example 5

Find T, the point which divides the line PQ joining P(–1, 5, 0) and Q(9, 0, 20) in the ratio 3:2.

Start with a sketch:

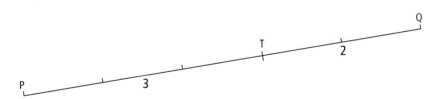

From the sketch, it is easy to see that $\frac{PT}{TQ} = \frac{3}{2}$ so that $2\overrightarrow{PT} = 3\overrightarrow{TQ}$.

Substituting position vectors, $\qquad 2(\mathbf{t} - \mathbf{p}) = 3(\mathbf{q} - \mathbf{t})$

After multiplying out and rearranging, this gives $\qquad 5\mathbf{t} = 2\mathbf{p} + 3\mathbf{q}$ (check it out for yourself).

From there, it is simple to substitute the components of **p** and **q** and solve to get $\quad \mathbf{t} = \begin{pmatrix} 5 \\ 2 \\ 12 \end{pmatrix}$

so that **T is the point (5, 2, 12)**.

You can use the formula $\mathbf{p} = \dfrac{n\mathbf{a} + m\mathbf{b}}{n + m}$ to find **p**, the position vector of P, the point which divides the line AB in the ratio m:n. Basically, it is a rearrangement of the procedure above into a neat formula. If you find it easier, you can use it with x, y and z components in turn instead of with the whole vector at once.

> **DON'T FORGET**
>
> Write: "$\overrightarrow{AC} = 4\overrightarrow{AB}$. So, AC is parallel to AB. And, since A is a common point, A, B and C are collinear points."

> **DON'T FORGET**
>
> It doesn't matter whether you use this formula or not – but you will have to know it if you are going to use it, because it doesn't appear in the exam formula list.

LET'S THINK ABOUT THIS

If, in example 5 above, you were asked to find S where $\overrightarrow{PS} = 2\overrightarrow{PQ}$, you would find a point lying outside the line PQ. Try sketching it and working out the coordinates of S.

VECTOR ALGEBRA – THE SCALAR PRODUCT

THE SCALAR PRODUCT

Here is how the scalar (or dot) product of two vectors **a** and **b** is calculated:

a.b = |**a**| |**b**| cos θ where θ is the angle between the vectors when they are placed nose-to-nose or tail-to-tail (both pointing in, or both pointing out).

The answer works out as a number, or scalar – not another vector – and it is straightforward to calculate it.

Example 6

Calculate **p.q** where |**p**| = 5, |**q**| = 4.

We must first rearrange the diagram so that both vectors point out.

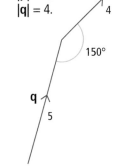

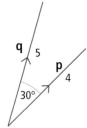

p.q $= 5 \times 4 \times \cos 30° = 20 \times \frac{\sqrt{3}}{2} = \mathbf{10\sqrt{3}}$

Particularly interesting cases are:

1 $\theta = 0°$ as, for example, **a.a** = |**a**| |**a**| cos 0° … Since cos 0° = 1, the result is **a.a** = |**a**|²

2 $\theta = 90°$ where the vectors are perpendicular. Since cos 90° = 0, the scalar product is then 0. This result is particularly handy in reverse – that is, if you find that a scalar product works out to be 0, the angle must be 90°, showing that the vectors are perpendicular.

The scalar product can also be worked out from components. This is also given in the exam formula list.

a.b = $a_1b_1 + a_2b_2 + a_3b_3$ (where a_1 etc. are vector components)

Here is an example of the calculation of the scalar product of two vectors:

$\begin{pmatrix} 3 \\ -1 \\ 2 \end{pmatrix} . \begin{pmatrix} 7 \\ 4 \\ -5 \end{pmatrix} = 3 \times 7 + (-1) \times 4 + 2 \times (-5) = 21 - 4 - 10 = 7$

If the vectors are given in component form, you should calculate their magnitudes first and then substitute into the formula which is given in the exam formula list.

Example 7

For what value of t is vector **p** = 3**i** – **j** + t**k** perpendicular to vector **q** = 2**i** + 3**j** – **k** ?

p.q = $3 \times 2 + -1 \times 3 + t \times -1 = 6 - 3 - t = 0$ for perpendicular vectors, hence $t = 3$.

What is really useful is not so much these results for the scalar product separately but what we can do by combining them.

$$\cos \theta = \frac{a_1b_1 + a_2b_2 + a_3b_3}{|\mathbf{a}| |\mathbf{b}|}$$

Substitute the vector components and calculate, and in no time at all you have found the angle between the vectors, as in this next example.

contd

THE SCALAR PRODUCT contd

Example 8

Find angle EPF in the cuboid diagram.

Worked out earlier: $\overrightarrow{PE} = \begin{pmatrix} 2 \\ 1 \\ 10 \end{pmatrix}$ $\overrightarrow{PF} = \begin{pmatrix} -3 \\ 1 \\ 10 \end{pmatrix}$

$\overrightarrow{PE}.\overrightarrow{PF} = 2 \times -3 + 1 \times 1 + 10 \times 10 = -6 + 1 + 100 = 95$

We already have $PF = \sqrt{110}$ and $PE = \sqrt{4 + 1 + 100} = \sqrt{105}$

$\cos \widehat{EPF} = \dfrac{\overrightarrow{PE}.\overrightarrow{PF}}{|\overrightarrow{PE}|\,|\overrightarrow{PF}|} = \dfrac{95}{\sqrt{105} \times \sqrt{110}} = 0{\cdot}8839 \ldots$

$\widehat{EPF} = \cos^{-1} 0{\cdot}8839 = \mathbf{27{\cdot}9°}$

DON'T FORGET

Be careful to note the directions of arrows on the diagrams.

VECTOR ALGEBRA

Some questions on vectors in the examination don't involve components or coordinates at all. They use the scalar product rule and two other vector results which you need to remember:

a.b = b.a   **a.(b + c) = a.b + a.c**

These questions will normally have some information about the lengths of vectors and angles between the vectors, possibly given with the help of a diagram. Vector paths can crop up too.

Example 9

Triangle ABC is equilateral with sides 3 units.

Evaluate **a.(b + c)** and determine the angle between vector **a** and the vector **b + c**

$\mathbf{a.(b + c)} = \mathbf{a.b} + \mathbf{a.c}$
$= |\mathbf{a}|\,|\mathbf{b}| \cos 60° + |\mathbf{a}|\,|\mathbf{c}| \cos 120°$ (remembering to place **a** and **c** "nose-to-nose")
$= 3 \times 3 \times 0{\cdot}5 + 3 \times 3 \times -0{\cdot}5$
$= 4{\cdot}5 - 4{\cdot}5 = \mathbf{0}$

Since the scalar product is 0, the angle between the vectors **a** and (**b + c**) is **90°**.

Example 10

In the diagram, PS:SR = 2:1, and vectors **u** and **v** are as indicated. Express QR in terms of **u** and **v**.

Notice first that $\overrightarrow{PS} = \overrightarrow{PQ} + \overrightarrow{QS} = \mathbf{u} + \mathbf{v}$

$\overrightarrow{QR} = \overrightarrow{QS} + \overrightarrow{SR}$
$= \overrightarrow{QS} + \tfrac{1}{2}\overrightarrow{PS}$
$= \mathbf{v} + \tfrac{1}{2}(\mathbf{u} + \mathbf{v})$
$= \tfrac{1}{2}\mathbf{u} + \tfrac{3}{2}\mathbf{v}$

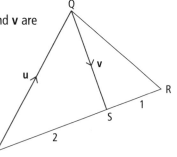

DON'T FORGET

Vector algebra questions may feature triangles that we know from the "exact value" table we use in trigonometry.

Example 11

Calculate **a.(a + b + c)**

$\mathbf{a.(a + b + c)} = \mathbf{a.a} + \mathbf{a.b} + \mathbf{a.c}$
$= 1 \times 1 + 1 \times 2 \cos 60° + 1 \times \sqrt{3} \times \cos 90°$
$= 1 + 2 \times \tfrac{1}{2} + 0$
$= \mathbf{2}$

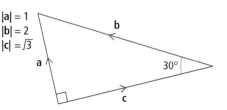

$|a| = 1$
$|b| = 2$
$|c| = \sqrt{3}$

$30°$

LET'S THINK ABOUT THIS

Asked to prove that ABCD is a rhombus A(14, –1), B(4, –1), C(–2, 7), D(8, 7), you would probably use techniques from the Straight Line topic. Can you do it instead using vectors, and without calculating any lengths?

SEQUENCES DEFINED BY RECURRENCE RELATIONS

A recurrence relation is a rule, or formula, given for working out any term in a sequence if you know the one before.

For example, with u_n standing for the *n*th term in a sequence, $u_{n+1} = u_n + 6$ (a recurrence relation) and $u_1 = -11$ (the first term) generates the infinite sequence –11, –5, 1, 7, 13, 19, 25, …

The recurrence relation

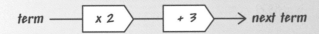

$$\text{term} \longrightarrow \boxed{\times 2} \longrightarrow \boxed{+3} \longrightarrow \text{next term}$$

is given by the formula $u_{n+1} = 2u_n + 3$

FORMULAE FOR SEQUENCES

FINDING TERMS IN A SEQUENCE

Given the formula and one term of a sequence, it is possible to find any others required.

Example 1

Using the formula above, and given that $u_3 = 5$, find **a** u_4 **b** u_6 **c** u_2

a $u_{n+1} = 2u_n + 3$
$u_4 = 2u_3 + 3$
$\quad = 2 \times 5 + 3 = \mathbf{13}$

b Do this twice more to get to u_6 … $u_5 = 29$, $u_6 = 61$

c Also from $\quad u_{n+1} = 2u_n + 3$
we can write $\quad u_3 = 2u_2 + 3$
$\quad\quad\quad\quad\quad 5 = 2u_2 + 3$
$\quad\quad\quad\quad\quad u_2 = 1$

Here is another important type of question:

Example 2

A sequence is defined by the linear recurrence relation $u_{n+1} = -4u_n + 7$
Express u_{n+2} in terms of u_n

From the recurrence relation, we can write $\quad u_{n+2} = -4u_{n+1} + 7$
and then we can substitute for u_{n+1}, obtaining $\quad u_{n+2} = -4(-4u_n + 7) + 7$
and then, simplifying the expression, $\quad u_{n+2} = \mathbf{16u_n - 21}$

USING A CALCULATOR

Evaluating terms is very easy with a calculator, though the questions on this topic are more often in Paper 1, where you won't have one.

key [5] [ENTER]
key [×] [2] [+] [3] [ENTER]
key [ENTER] for more terms …

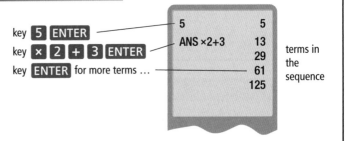

terms in the sequence

FINDING THE FORMULA FOR A SEQUENCE FROM GIVEN TERMS

With at least three terms, you can use simultaneous equations to find a formula

$$u_{n+1} = au_n + b$$

Example 3

Find the values of a and b in the sequence defined by $u_{n+1} = au_n + b$
where $u_3 = -1$, $u_4 = -9$ and $u_5 = -41$

Using the three terms given, we can write: $u_4 = au_3 + b$
and substitute to obtain $-9 = -a - b$
and $u_5 = au_4 + b$
substitute $-41 = -9a - b$

Solve the pair of equations in a and b simultaneously:

Subtracting the second from the first gives $32 = 8a$ and so **$a = 4$**

Substituting 4 for a in equation 1 gives **$b = -5$** and the recurrence relation is $u_{n+1} = 4u_n - 5$

SETTING UP SEQUENCES FROM REAL-LIFE CONTEXTS

Examples from "real life" include growth and decay, bank loans, pollution levels, inflation, policies for culling animals, removing pests and monitoring drug levels in patients. They normally involve changes over time – for example, a patient may be given a dose of antibiotic *every four hours*, or interest may be added to a loan *every month*. Use a "0" suffix for the amount at the start (A_0 rather than A_1) because then A_4 will mean the value after four of these time intervals. This avoids confusion!

Percentage increases and decreases often feature:
16% increase means that, after each interval, we have
original 100% + 16% = 116%   so × 1·16 to get new value.

9% decrease means that, after each interval, we have
original 100% − 9% = 81%   so × 0·81 to get new value.

Example 4

Snow covers the ski slopes of Mont Gris to a depth of 170 cm at noon, but it is melting at a rate of 15% every hour. Will the snow depth remain over 1 metre until skiing stops at 4pm?

$S_0 = 170$ 15% melts, so 85% remains – multiplier is 0·85

Set up the recurrence relation: $S_n = 0\cdot85 \times S_{n-1}$

S_n stands for the depth of snow after n hours, so for the snow at 4pm we need S_4

$S_1 = 0\cdot85\, S_0$
$S_2 = 0\cdot85\, S_1 = 0\cdot85 \times 0\cdot85\, S_0 = 0\cdot85^2\, S_0$
$S_3 = 0\cdot85\, S_2 = 0\cdot85 \times 0\cdot85^2\, S_0 = 0\cdot85^3\, S_0$
So, following the pattern,
$S_4 = 0\cdot85^4\, S_0 = 0\cdot85^4 \times 170\,cm$
= **89 cm approx.**

Hence the snow cover **does** fall below 1 metre.

DON'T FORGET

Examples with percentages are more likely to be set in Paper 2, where you will have your calculator.

DON'T FORGET

You do not need to write all this down – it's here in case anyone reading this has forgotten how it works!

DON'T FORGET

This example can be worked out this way because there is no "add a constant" part in the formula. Keying it in as a recurrence relation will take scarcely any more time, however.

LET'S THINK ABOUT THIS

Make up a sequence where $u_{n+1} = u_n + 1$ (where these two easily confused expressions **are** actually the same).

LIMITS OF A SEQUENCE

With some sequences, the terms become closer and closer to a fixed value, called the limit of the sequence. This is called convergence. For other sequences, the terms diverge.

For example, 5, 2, 1·4, 1·28, 1·56, 1·2512, 1·25024, … converges to 1·25

whereas 5, 11, 23, 47, 95, 191, … diverges.

DON'T FORGET

If you are asked whether or not a sequence has a limit, or are asked to prove that a limit exists, it is not enough to state simply what the limit is. You must identify what "a" is in the recurrence relation and then state that $-1 < "a" < 1$.

WHEN DOES A LIMIT EXIST?

The terms of a sequence generated by a recurrence relation $u_n = au_{n-1} + b$ will converge to a limit if $-1 < a < 1$.

For example, the convergent sequence above comes from the recurrence relation $u_{n+1} = 0\cdot2\, u_n + 1$. This means that a, the multiplier, is $0\cdot2$.

A limit exists because $-1 < 0\cdot2 < 1$ and this must be stated in the answer.

DON'T FORGET

Whichever method you choose to use to find the limit (denoted by L), you need to remember it, as they are not given in the exam formula list.

FINDING THE LIMIT OF A SEQUENCE

There are two ways to set out the working for this, and different teachers may prefer one or the other. Both are used in this section, but stick with the way you were taught unless you have a good reason to change.

A convergent sequence has a limit L, then … $L = aL + b$

Using this to find the limit for the example in the section above,
$$u_{n+1} = 0\cdot2\, u_n + 1$$
substituting …
$$L = 0\cdot2\, L + 1$$
$$L - 0\cdot2L = 1$$
$$0\cdot8L = 1$$
$$L = \frac{1}{0\cdot8} = \frac{10}{8} = \frac{5}{4}$$

Alternatively, you can use $L = \frac{b}{1-a} = \frac{1}{1-0\cdot2} = \frac{1}{0\cdot8} = \frac{5}{4}$
which leads to exactly the same fraction calculation – there's no avoiding it!

You have to be able to calculate limits like this without a calculator. The arithmetic needed is quite elementary (multiply both numerator and denominator by a number which will make them both whole numbers before trying to simplify), but not all Higher candidates are competent in this. Practise if you are one of them.

Example 5

The sequence $u_{n+1} = ku_n + 1\cdot2$ tends to a limit of 3 as $n \to \infty$.

Determine the value of k.

Using $L = \frac{b}{1-a}$ we can substitute for L and b and solve for a.
$$L = \frac{b}{1-a}$$
$$3 = \frac{1\cdot2}{1-k}$$
$$3(1-k) = 1\cdot2$$
$$3k = 1\cdot8$$
$$k = 0\cdot6$$

DON'T FORGET

$n \to \infty$ means "n tends to infinity", which simply means it gets bigger without limit.

contd

FINDING THE LIMIT OF A SEQUENCE contd

Example 6

The following two recurrence relations generate sequences with the same limit:

(1) $P_{n+1} = aP_n + 4$
(2) $Q_{n+1} = a^2Q_n + 2$

Find the value of a and evaluate the limit.

Solution

Find expressions for the limits of both formulae and equate them:

$L_1 = \dfrac{b}{1-a} = \dfrac{4}{1-a}$

$L_2 = \dfrac{b}{1-a} = \dfrac{2}{1-a^2}$ so $\dfrac{4}{1-a} = \dfrac{2}{1-a^2}$

Solve this equation:
$$2(1-a) = 4(1-a^2)$$
$$2 - 2a = 4 - 4a^2$$
$$4a^2 - 2a - 2 = 0$$
$$(2a-2)(2a+1) = 0$$
$$a = 1 \quad a = -0.5$$

since $-1 < a < 1$ for a limit to exist, $a = -0.5$

Evaluating the limit for this value,

$$L = \dfrac{4}{1-(-0.5)} = \dfrac{4}{1.5} = \dfrac{8}{3}$$

Limit is $\dfrac{8}{3}$

> **DON'T FORGET**
>
> You must always check whether a solution for **a** lies in the range $-1 < a < 1$.

Example 7

a Pondweed is present in a pond and spreads during the summer growth period over a further 20 square metres. A team of volunteers clears 20% of the pondweed in an annual clean-up in the winter. If this volunteer work continues at the same rate, what area of the pond will be covered with pondweed each winter before the annual clean-up in the long term?

b The council decides that this amount of pondweed is still unsightly and decides to employ a team to clear the pond each winter so that the pondweed after each clean-up does not cover more than 40 sq m of the pond. What percentage of the pondweed needs to be removed annually to achieve this target?

a Before the annual clean-up:

$A_n = 0.8A_{n-1} + 20$ (20% removed; 80% remains, 20 sq m extra during year).

Since $-1 < 0.8 < 1$, there will be a limit to the amount of pondweed in the long term.

Using $L = aL + b$ to find the limit, $L = 0.8L + 20$
$$0.2L = 20$$
$$L = \dfrac{20}{0.2} = \dfrac{200}{2} = 100$$

The pondweed will cover **100 sq** m in the long term.

b We need the value of a which gives the formula $A_n = aA_n + 20$ a limit of 40.

Substitute in the limit formula: $L = \dfrac{b}{1-a}$
$$40 = \dfrac{20}{1-a}$$
$$40 - 40a = 20$$
leading to $a = 0.5$.

This means that **50%** must be removed (so, 50% remains) at each clean-up.

> **DON'T FORGET**
>
> You must watch out for examples like this where the percentage in the question (20% here) is *not* the percentage you use for the calculations! (80%)

LET'S THINK ABOUT THIS

What about the convergence/divergence of the sequence in example 1 (see p24) – and what does the value of "a" have to do with it?

FUNCTIONS AND GRAPHS

We deal with a great many graphs in Higher – parabolas, exponentials, cubics, sine and other trig functions, not to mention the simple straight line. We also deal with rules, formulae or equations (different words can be used) linking the x and y-coordinates of the points on graphs.

An understanding of the relationship between *formulae* and *graphs* of functions at the beginning of this chapter is helpful for many questions throughout the exam paper, but also to answering some of the short questions in the exam. Later in the chapter, quadratic and polynomial functions are revised.

Rules can be given as $y = \ldots$ or $f(x) = \ldots$

FORMULAE, DOMAIN AND RANGE

RELATING GRAPHS AND FORMULAE

Here is a question on relating a graph to its formula.

Example 1

The diagram shows part of the graph whose equation is of the form $y = 3p^x$

What is the value of *p*?

Frequently, a problem can be solved simply by substituting coordinates of a known point into the equation, as here:

substitute $x = 3$ and $y = 24$ $24 = 3p^3$
$$p^3 = 8 \text{ so } \mathbf{p = 2}$$

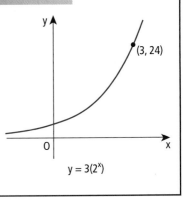

(3, 24)

$y = 3(2^x)$

DOMAIN AND RANGE

You need to know what these words mean:
    Domain – the set of values for **inputs** for the function (**x**-values)
    Range – the set of values calculated by the function for the **outputs** (y-values)
    Mostly **R – the set of real numbers** – is both domain and range.

Two situations where the domain may need to be restricted:
1 Square-root functions – because you can't find the square root of a negative, or indeed any even-numbered root of a negative, for example $4\sqrt{-16}$.
2 Functions involving division – because you cannot divide by zero.

Example 2

What domain is most suitable for $f(x) = \sqrt{x^2 - 4}$?

$x^2 - 4 \geq 0 \Rightarrow x^2 \geq 4 \Rightarrow x \geq 2, \ x \leq -2$

This can be shown as a subset of R on a number line.

The solution to the inequality is two separate sections of the real number line.

Looking a little more at inequalities, notice that the solution to the inequality $x^2 < 9$ is $\mathbf{x < 3}$ and $\mathbf{x > -3}$. When the values satisfying these conditions are marked on a number line, it is **one** continuous section, hence it can be described in **one** inequality statement $\mathbf{-3 < x < 3}$.

Notice that, in such cases, we always write it starting with the smaller value and increasing to the larger.

contd

DOMAIN AND RANGE   contd

Example 3

What domain is most suitable for
$g(x) = \frac{x^2}{5 - 3x}$?

Solve $5 - 3x = 0$ (to find the value
of x which makes the denominator 0)
$$3x = 5$$
$$x = \frac{5}{3}$$
The domain is $x \in R, x \neq \frac{5}{3}$

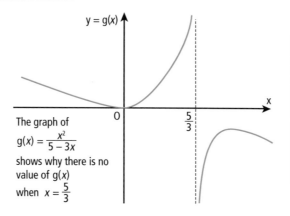

The graph of
$g(x) = \frac{x^2}{5 - 3x}$
shows why there is no
value of $g(x)$
when $x = \frac{5}{3}$

> **DON'T FORGET**
>
> Looking at the graph of a function, you can spot values missing from the domain because the graph will be **discontinuous** there – as in the graph shown.

When it comes to the range of a function, a value can only be in the range if it can be obtained as an "output" for one of the possible inputs of the function. For example, the function $y = x^2$ cannot produce any negative values whatever value of x is chosen, so there are no negative values in the range. The range is $y \geq 0$.

Example 4

What is the range of the function $f(x) = 3 - x^2$?

Looking at the graph of the function, there are no solutions when $f(x) > 3$, so the range is

$f(x) \leq 3$.

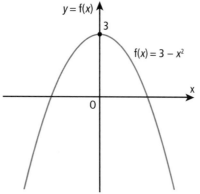

> **DON'T FORGET**
>
> Provided you have a graph, you will see that scanning it horizontally (for the domain) or vertically (for the range) will show where there are excluded values.

The next example asks us to consider just a section of a graph, by giving a domain restriction to indicate that f(x) is only defined for certain values of x.

Example 5

Find the greatest and least values of the function
$f(x) = x^3 - 12x - 16$ on the interval $-2 \leq x \leq 3$

Think of vertical lines being placed through the graph at $x = 3$ and $x = -2$. It's obvious that the highest point reached by the graph between these lines is 0 (when $x = -2$). It looks as if $x = 2$ is a minimum turning point, in which case the lowest value of the graph will be there.

Differentiating, $\frac{dy}{dx} = 3x^2 - 12 = 3(x^2 - 4)$
for stationary points $\frac{dy}{dx} = 0$
$\Rightarrow x = 2, -2$ … so yes, there **is** a minimum at 2.

When $x = 2$, $y = 2^3 - 12 \times 2 - 16 = -32$

The greatest value of the function is 0 and the least is –32.

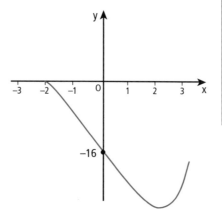

> **DON'T FORGET**
>
> In any exam questions, the greatest and least values within an interval will occur either at the endpoints or at turning points on the graph.

LET'S THINK ABOUT THIS

What feature on the graph of $y = \frac{1}{x}$ stops it from being a suitable graph for which to find the greatest and least values in the interval $-1 < x < 1$?

TRANSFORMATIONS OF GRAPHS

TRANSFORMATION IN THE y-DIRECTION

There are certain alterations to the formula for a function which will transform the graph of the function in a predictable way.

1 If a constant is added to f(x), the whole graph moves up.

Adding a negative will result in the graph moving down.

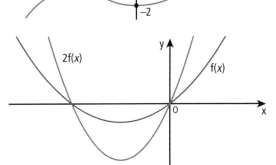

2 If f(x) is multiplied by a constant, the graph stretches away from the x-axis.

Each individual point moves k times further away from the x-axis to give this stretching effect because its y-coordinate is multiplied by k.

When k is negative, the graph stretches away from the x-axis in the opposite direction.

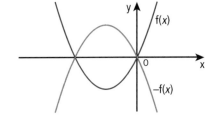

If $k = -1$, the graph will not be stretched but it will still be in the opposite direction – it will be a **reflection in the x-axis**.

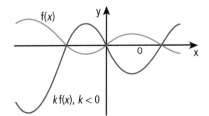

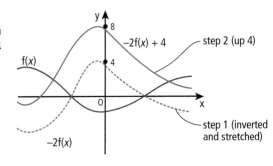

When $0 < k < 1$, the graph is compressed instead of stretched.

Example 6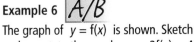

The graph of $y = f(x)$ is shown. Sketch and annotate the graph $y = -2f(x) + 4$

−2 will invert the graph **and** stretch it vertically by a factor of 2 (shown on the diagram as a dotted line).

+4 will move the dotted line graph up 4 units (shown in blue).

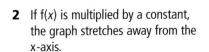

Example 7

The graph of g(x) is as shown in blue on the diagram. Write the formula for the second graph, shown in red, in terms of g(x).

Both graphs cut the x-axis at the same points, so the graph has not been moved up. It has been stretched. Looking at the maximum and minimum turning points, we can see they are three times as far up or down on the red graph as on the blue. The stretch factor is 3, and the formula is $y = 3g(x)$.

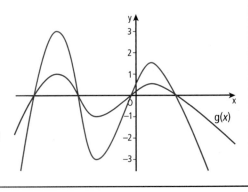

TRANSFORMATION IN THE X-DIRECTION

The alteration in the graph will be in the horizontal direction if it is x which is added to, or x which is multiplied, rather than the whole formula for f(x).

1 Adding a constant to x moves the graph to the **left if the constant is positive** (shown in yellow) and to the **right if it is negative** (shown in green).

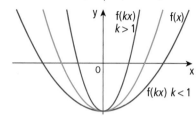

2 Multiplying by a constant compresses the graph horizontally – in the x-direction (shown in blue). If the constant is fractional, the graph is stretched (shown in red).

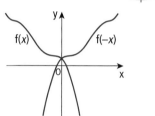

3 Multiplying x by −1 gives a **reflection in the y-axis**.

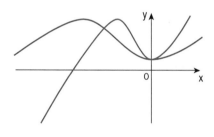

Example 8

The graph of f(x) is shown along with the graph of $y = $ f($2x$).

Which is which?

In the transformed graph, all the points must be half as far away from the vertical axis. Thus **f(x) is the graph shown in red, and f($2x$) is in blue.**

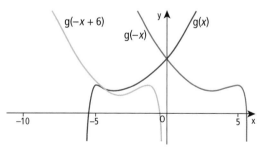

Example 9 $\boxed{A/B}$

The graph shows $y = $ g(x).
Sketch the graph of g($6 − x$).

Rearranging the formula gives g($−x + 6$), revealing that the transformation is a reflection in the y-axis and a shift of 6 to the left.

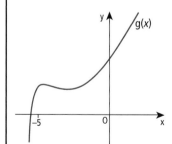

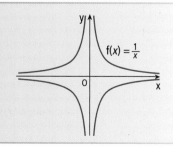

LET'S THINK ABOUT THIS

The section of graph in the first quadrant is part of the graph of
$$f(x) = \frac{1}{x}$$
Use the transformation-of-graphs techniques to establish the equations of the other three sections of graph.

QUADRATIC FUNCTION AND GRAPH

USING GRAPH TRANSFORMATIONS TO ESTABLISH EQUATIONS OF QUADRATICS

To draw the graph of $y = h(x - 3) - 2$, given the graph of $h(x)$, the graph of $h(x)$ is moved 3 to the right and down 2.

The graph is a parabola, with turning point $(3, -2)$.

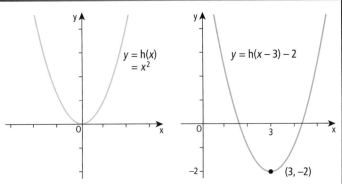

Now, if you are also told that $h(x) = x^2$, which you can see will fit the sketch, you can also give the equation of the transformed graph in standard quadratic form:

$$y = h(x - 3)^2 - 2$$
$$= (x - 3)^2 - 2$$
$$= x^2 - 6x + 9 - 2$$
$$= x^2 - 6x + 7$$

This is obviously a very handy way to get the equation of a quadratic graph from a sketch where you can read off the coordinates of the turning point easily – but we mustn't get too carried away just yet. All the graphs in this next diagram are quadratic functions which turn at $(3, -2)$, but they obviously can't all have the same equation, $y = x^2 - 6x + 7$

However, they are all variations of $y = (x - 3)^2 - 2$

They have equations $y = \mathbf{k}(x - 3)^2 - 2$ for different values of k

For example, blue graph is
$$y = -(x - 3)^2 - 2$$
$$= -x^2 + 6x - 11$$
red graph is
$$y = 2(x - 3)^2 - 2$$
$$= 2x^2 - 12x + 16$$
and they can be obtained from $y = (x - 3)^2 - 2$ (shown in green) by using transformations already discussed in this chapter.

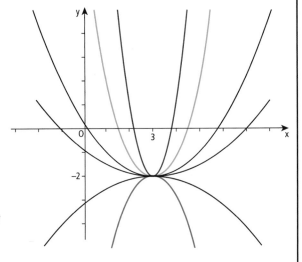

It's necessary to have another point on the graph given to decide which equation fits. Often, the intercept on the y-axis will do.

"COMPLETING THE SQUARE" TO FIND FORMULAS FOR QUADRATIC FUNCTIONS

There's some serious algebra involved in finding the equation of a graph from its turning point, and so exam questions often work the other way round – starting with the equation, you are asked to rearrange it in order to identify the turning point. This is much easier, especially as the question usually gives you hints for the algebra.

It's important that you have spotted an important connection when "squaring brackets":

$(x - k)^2 = x^2 - 2kx \ldots$

For example, $(x + 5)^2 = x^2 + 10x$ and $(x - 2)^2 = x^2 - 4x \ldots$

The coefficient of the x term is double the constant in the bracket.

Example 11

a Express $x^2 + 8x - 1$ in the form $(x + a)^2 + b$
b State the coordinates of the turning point of the graph of $y = x^2 + 8x - 1$
c Sketch the curve, indicating the y-intercept.

From the above, we know $x^2 + 8x - 1 = (x + 4)^2$ plus something as the coefficient of the x term is double the constant in the bracket.

Since $(x + 4)^2 = x^2 + 8x + 16$

we can see that $x^2 + 8x - 1 = (x^2 + 8x + 16) - 17 = (x + 4)^2 - 17$

This shows us (using graph transformations) that the graph is $y = x^2$ moved 4 to the left and down 17, so the minimum turning point is $(-4, -17)$.

To sketch the curve, we need also to know how steeply it slopes – so, calculate another point from its equation. Putting 0 in the place of x, we get $y = 0^2 + 8 \times 0 - 1 = -1$ (actually, you should spot that without needing to do the substitution …), so we have $(0, -1)$ on the y-axis.

There is a more systematic way to rearrange a quadratic equation. If you can't spot the rearrangement by inspection (just by looking), then use this method of equating coefficients.

Example 12

Express $3x^2 - 12x + 17$ in the form $3(x - a)^2 + b$ and write down the turning point of the parabola with equation $y = 3x^2 - 12x + 17$

Multiply out:
$3(x - a)^2 + b$
$= 3(x^2 - 2ax + a^2) + b$
$= 3x^2 - 6ax + 3a^2 + b$

Now we have:
$3x^2 - 12x + 17 = 3x^2 - 6ax + 3a^2 + b$

Equating x terms, we have:
$-12x = -6ax$ so $a = 2$

and, equating constants, we have: $17 = 3a^2 + b$
$= 3 \times 2^2 + b$
$= 12 + b$
So, $b = 5$

so $3x^2 - 12x + 17 = 3(x - 2)^2 + 5$ and the turning point is $(2, 5)$.

For a level C example, use this method to do Example 11.

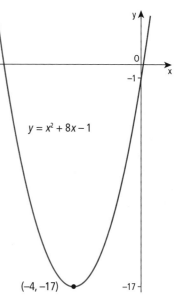

$y = x^2 + 8x - 1$

$(-4, -17)$

(2, 5)

DON'T FORGET

This "by inspection" method relies on you spotting what the brackets will be to fit the x terms. Always check that, when multiplied out, your rearrangement is exactly the same as the original quadratic expression.

DON'T FORGET

Equating coefficients is a very **reliable** way of finding unknown constants in quadratic equations. It's a particularly good idea in examples like the one here, where there is a constant in front of the $(x \ldots)$ bracket. The constant must always be taken out of the bracket in such cases.

 LET'S THINK ABOUT THIS

Can you work out what three transformations would be necessary to change the graph of $y = x^2$ into the one in example 12?

SOLUTION OF QUADRATIC EQUATIONS

ZEROS OF THE QUADRATIC FUNCTION

DON'T FORGET

The formula works perfectly well for rational roots also, but is an unnecessarily cumbersome method if factorisation is possible. However, should you find yourself unable to find factors quickly, the formula is a good stand-by.

The zeros of the quadratic function are the x-coordinates of the points where the graph cuts the x-axis. There could be two, one or none at all.

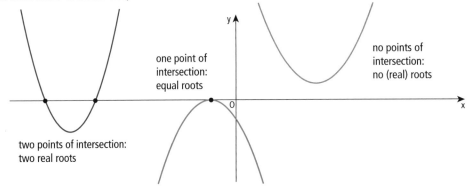

one point of intersection: equal roots

no points of intersection: no (real) roots

two points of intersection: two real roots

For a parabola $y = ax^2 + bx + c$ the zeros are the roots (where they exist) of the quadratic equation $ax^2 + bx + c = 0$

Factorisation is the simplest method for solving quadratic equations, but only works for rational roots such as 2, –5, $\frac{3}{7}$ and so on, and not for irrational roots such as 3·89625…

For irrational roots, the quadratic formula on p. 36 is the usual method.

Of course, you will have come across the methods of solving quadratics before you began the Higher course, but Higher takes the solutions of quadratic equations to new levels.

SOLUTION OF QUADRATIC EQUATIONS BY FACTORISATION

DON'T FORGET

It's well worth going the extra mile to give the examiner exactly what is wanted: if points are asked for, then stopping at the roots –2 and –3 just isn't a good idea – marks may well be deducted!

DON'T FORGET

Why no calculator for the working? At Higher, it is important that you can demonstrate good numerical skills. You could be asked to do a fractions calculation of this difficulty in Paper 1, though more complex examples would be in Paper 2 and could be done with the help of your calculator.

Example 13

Find the coordinates of the points where the graph $y = x^2 + 5x + 6$ cuts the x-axis and the coordinates and nature of the turning point.

Solve $x^2 + 5x + 6 = 0$
$(x + 2)(x + 3) = 0$
$x = -2$, $x = -3$ giving points **(–2, 0) and (–3, 0)**.

By symmetry, the turning point occurs midway between the roots, where $x = -2\frac{1}{2}$

Calculate y:

$y = (-\frac{5}{2})^2 + 5 \times (-\frac{5}{2}) + 6$

$\quad = \frac{25}{4} - \frac{25}{2} + 6$

$\quad = 6 - 6\frac{1}{4}$

$\quad = -\frac{1}{4}$

The turning point is $(-2\frac{1}{2}, -\frac{1}{4})$.

It is a minimum turning point since the coefficient of the x^2 term is positive (an attempt to sketch the graph will convince you if you aren't sure why).

FINDING THE EQUATION OF A QUADRATIC FUNCTION FROM ITS ROOTS

Example 14

What is the equation of the graph?

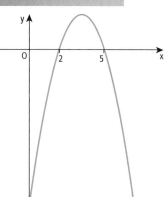

From the zeros of the function, we can work backwards:

$x = 2$ and $x = 5$ lead back to:
$y = k(x - 2)(x - 5)$ (k is necessary because there is not just one parabola with those zeros.)

To find k, substitute in the coordinates of a known point:

$x = 0$, $y = -20$ (this is the only other point we have)
$-20 = k \times -2 \times -5$
$-10k = 20$
$k = -2$

so, the equation of the graph is $y = -2(x - 2)(x - 5)$ or $\mathbf{y = -2x^2 + 14x - 20}$

> **DON'T FORGET**
>
> In the exam, you will probably be given the form of the equation, complete with "k" if necessary, to help you.

SOLVING QUADRATIC INEQUATIONS

You also have to be able to solve quadratic *inequations* (or *inequalities*). Think of this as finding the part of the graph above or below the x-axis. It's generally a good idea to solve the corresponding *equation* first, which will give the values for which $y = 0$, where the graph would cut the x-axis.

> **DON'T FORGET**
>
> Always take care as to whether an inequality has $<$ or $\leq$ and make sure you follow through.

Example 15

Solve $x^2 + 5x - 24 < 0$

First, solve $x^2 + 5x - 24 = 0$. Factors of 24 could be $2,12$ $3,8$ $4,6$ or even $1,24$ but a little experimentation with the middle term leads us to 3 and 8:

$(x + 8)(x - 3) = 0$
$x = -8$, $x = 3$

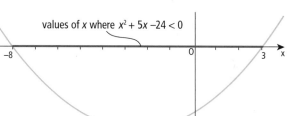

values of x where $x^2 + 5x - 24 < 0$

Now sketch the parabola (on paper or mentally) $y = x^2 + 5x - 24$ which is U-shaped. Remember that we only need to know where $y < 0$ (in other words, the range of values for x for which the graph is below the x-axis).

We can see from the diagram that $x^2 + 5x - 24 < 0$ when $\mathbf{-8 < x < 3}$

ROOTS OF QUADRATIC EQUATIONS BY METHOD OF COMPLETING THE SQUARE

Example 16

To remind you of completing the square as a method, which is a useful skill for Higher even if not often the easiest way to solve a quadratic equation, let's solve $x^2 + 8x - 1 = 0$.

$x^2 + 8x - 1 = 0$
$(x + 4)^2 - 17 = 0$ (as already found in example 11)
$(x + 4)^2 = 17$
$x + 4 = \pm\sqrt{17}$
$x = -4 + \sqrt{17}$, $-4 - \sqrt{17}$
$\mathbf{x = 0{\cdot}12, -8{\cdot}12}$ **correct to 2 dp**

✿ LET'S THINK ABOUT THIS

Finding roots of a quadratic equation proves that roots exist (assuming the maths has been done correctly, of course). On the other hand, does *not* finding roots prove they *don't* exist?

QUADRATIC FORMULA AND THE DISCRIMINANT

THE QUADRATIC FORMULA

If the method of completing the square was used to solve the equation

$ax^2 + bx + c = 0$, the answers would be $x = \dfrac{-b \pm \sqrt{b^2 - 4ac}}{2a}$ $a \neq 0$

which neatly sums up how to find the roots of any quadratic equation by substituting its coefficients in the result in place of a, b and c.

Example 17

Solve $3 + 2p - 2p^2 = 0$

First, $a = -2$, $b = 2$ and $c = 3$

Substituting into the quadratic formula: $x = \dfrac{-2 \pm \sqrt{2^2 - 4 \times (-2) \times 3}}{-4}$

$= \dfrac{-2 \pm \sqrt{28}}{-4}$

leading to $x = -0{\cdot}82$ **and** $x = 1{\cdot}82$ **(2 dp)**.

If you need practice, a more exciting way might be to make up some quadratic equations for yourself, solve them and check by graphing each function on a graphic calculator. The less exciting way is to find a textbook full of examples.

USING THE DISCRIMINANT $b^2 - 4ac$

The work in Higher is not so much about using the quadratic formula to find roots but about deciding the **nature** of the roots. It is the **discriminant**, $b^2 - 4ac$, which decides this:

$b^2 - 4ac > 0$ two distinct roots

$b^2 - 4ac = 0$ two equal real roots, or one (repeated) real root

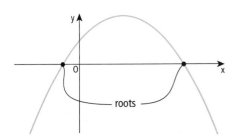

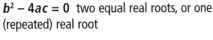

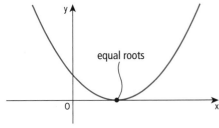

$b^2 - 4ac \geq 0$ for real roots
$b^2 - 4ac < 0$ no real roots

Example 18

Find the nature of the roots of $x^2 + 8x - 1 = 0$

First find a, b and c: $a = 1$ $b = 8$ $c = -1$

$b^2 - 4ac = 8^2 - 4 \times 1 \times (-1) = 64 + 4 = 68$

Since $b^2 - 4ac > 0$, roots are real and unequal.

Questions are not usually as straightforward as that one, however.

contd

USING THE DISCRIMINANT $b^2 - 4ac$ contd

Example 19

Find the range of values of k so that $kx^2 + x - 1 = 0$ has no real roots.

Identify a, b and c: $a = k$ $b = 1$ $c = -1$

Substitute these into the discriminant: $b^2 - 4ac = 1^2 - 4 \times k \times (-1)$

For no real roots, $b^2 - 4ac < 0 \Rightarrow 1 + 4k < 0$
$$4k > 1$$
$$k > \tfrac{1}{4}$$

Example 20

Show that the roots of $3x^2 + px - 2 = 0$ are real for all values of p.

$b^2 - 4ac = p^2 + 12$ Since $p^2 > 0$ for all p, $p^2 + 12 > 12$ for all p

Hence **$b^2 - 4ac > 0$ for all p, and so the roots are real.**

DON'T FORGET

For the purposes of Higher, "no real roots" means "no roots". You don't have to think about what roots that aren't real might be – but, if you are interested, read the "Let's think about this" at the foot of the page.

TANGENTS TO A CURVE

Sometimes, it might not be so obvious that the discriminant is relevant in a question.

Example 21

Show that the line $y = 5 - 4x$ does not intersect the parabola $y = x^2 - 6x + 7$

Points of intersection would have the same coordinates, so:

$$x^2 - 6x + 7 = 5 - 4x \text{ (equating the } y\text{-coordinates)}$$
leading to $x^2 - 2x + 2 = 0$ a quadratic equation!

The existence or otherwise of points of intersection is going to depend on whether or not that equation has solutions – and that depends on what the discriminant is.

$b^2 - 4ac = (-2)^2 - 4 \times 1 \times 2 = 4 - 8 = -4$

Since $b^2 - 4ac < 0$ there are no solutions, so the line and the parabola do not intersect (like the first diagram below).

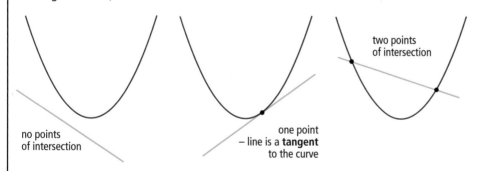

no points of intersection

one point – line is a **tangent** to the curve

two points of intersection

DON'T FORGET

Two solutions …
$b^2 - 4ac > 0$ …
line cuts parabola twice.

One solution …
$b^2 - 4ac = 0$ …
line meets parabola once – a *tangent*.

Where the discriminant is not negative and so there are solutions, solving the quadratic equation, by one of the methods given, will find them.

LET'S THINK ABOUT THIS

We say "no real roots" (when the discriminant works out as, for example, $\sqrt{-17}$) rather than "no roots".

You can't place $\sqrt{-17}$) even approximately on the real-number line, but if you study maths beyond Higher you will learn to denote $\sqrt{-1}$) by i (for "imaginary") and study the mathematics of "complex numbers" such as $3i$ and $2 - 7i$.

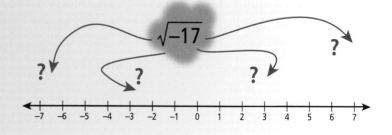

POLYNOMIAL FUNCTIONS

FACTORISING POLYNOMIALS – SYNTHETIC DIVISION METHOD

DON'T FORGET

Since $x^0 = 1$, 18 can be written as $18x^0$, thus revealing itself to be a power of x too.

Here is a polynomial function of degree 3 – a cubic function:

$$f(x) = x^3 + 2x^2 - 21x + 18$$

It contains different powers of x, with 3 being the highest power.

Just like quadratics (polynomials of degree 2), polynomials can often be factorised, and from their factors we can find roots which tell us where the graph of the polynomial cuts the x-axis. At the most, the number of real roots is the same as the degree.

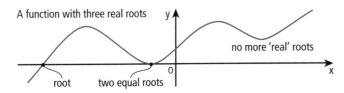

A function with three real roots

no more 'real' roots

root   two equal roots

The graph of a polynomial function is a continuous line. It can meander up and down, but it must keep moving from left to right as it does so.

DON'T FORGET

When working with polynomials, it's better to have them arranged in descending (or ascending) order of powers – not randomly – and to notice where there are "missing" powers.

Once we get beyond quadratics, we need better techniques for finding factors.

This particular cubic can be factorised into linear factors:

$$x^3 + 2x^2 - 21x + 18 = (x - a)(x - b)(x - c)$$

We need a bit of inspiration to find one factor. Finding the others will then be easier.

Obviously, we can't get 18 for the constant term if we multiply numbers like 5 or 7. a, b and c will all have to be factors of 18, $\pm 1, \pm 2, \pm 3, \pm 6, \pm 9, \pm 18$

Very important result: if $f(x)$ is divided by $(x - a)$, the remainder is $f(a)$.

If $(x - 3)$ is a *factor* of our polynomial, $f(3) = 0$ (no remainder for a factor).

Let's evaluate: $f(3) = 3^3 + 2 \times 3^2 - 21 \times 3 + 18 = 0$ so $(x - 3)$ *is* a factor.

(If we hadn't got 0, then another number would have to be tried instead.)

So, $x^3 + 2x^2 - 21x + 18 = (x - 3)$(a quadratic factor).

DON'T FORGET

This trial-and-error way of spotting and testing for a factor works well. Make sure you record what you've tried.

Probably the simplest way to find the quadratic factor is by *synthetic division*, although you might have another way you prefer. (If so, you can use your method each time for the rest of this section.) Synthetic division is just a procedure which gives the *quotient* (the "answer") and the *remainder* when we divide by $(x - 3)$.

Very important – it is because the remainder, $f(3)$, is zero that $(x - 3)$ is a factor.

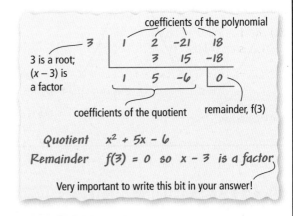

coefficients of the polynomial

3 is a root; $(x - 3)$ is a factor

coefficients of the quotient   remainder, $f(3)$

Quotient $x^2 + 5x - 6$

Remainder $f(3) = 0$ so $x - 3$ is a factor

Very important to write this bit in your answer!

DON'T FORGET

Synthetic division can be used to factorise polynomial expressions of degree higher than 3 by exactly the same method. For a polynomial of degree 4, you would use it twice until you have a quadratic quotient, at which point you revert to inspection as in the example here.

As the quotient is a quadratic, there is no need to use synthetic division to continue the factorisation. We can factorise $x^2 + 5x - 6$ by inspection:

$$x^2 + 5x - 6 = (x + 6)(x - 1)$$

So $f(x) = (x - 3)(x + 6)(x - 1)$

USING THE GRAPH OF A POLYNOMIAL FUNCTION TO FIND ITS FORMULA

Example 22

Find an expression for f(x), the function whose roots are $x = -5$, $x = -2$ and $x = 1$ and which cuts the y-axis at $(0, -20)$.

The roots -5, -2 and 1 mean there are factors $(x + 5)$, $(x + 2)$ and $(x - 1)$, so
f(x) $= k(x + 5)(x + 2)(x - 1)$

Substitute $(0, -20)$: $-20 = k \times 5 \times 2 \times -1$ so $k = 2$

Multiply out: f(x) $= 2(x + 5)(x^2 + x - 2) = \mathbf{2x^3 + 12x^2 + 6x - 20}$

MORE FACTORISATION OF POLYNOMIAL FUNCTIONS

It might be necessary to use synthetic division with a factor like $(2x + 1)$.

Example 23

Show that $(2x + 1)$ is a factor of
f(x) $= 2x^3 - 9x^2 + x + 3$ and state the other factor.

We need to rewrite $2x + 1$ as $2(x + \frac{1}{2})$ and
divide f(x) by $(x + \frac{1}{2})$.

The synthetic division gives **remainder 0, so
$(x + \frac{1}{2})$ is a factor**.

(Always remember to state in your answer that
there is a factor *because the remainder is zero*.)

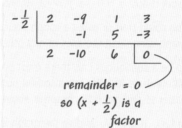

remainder = 0
so $(x + \frac{1}{2})$ is a
factor

So, f(x) $= (x + \frac{1}{2})(2x^2 - 10x + 6)$ … but this now needs some rearrangement:

   f(x) $= (x + \frac{1}{2}) \times 2(x^2 - 5x + 3)$ … removing the factor 2 from second bracket

      $= (2x + 1)(x^2 - 5x + 3)$ … and putting it back in the first,

so the other factor is $(x^2 - 5x + 3)$ (note that this doesn't factorise).

Example 24

$(x - 2)$ is a factor of f(x) $= x^3 + px - 2$. Find the value of p and factorise the cubic expression fully.

f(2) could be calculated and put equal to zero, but we also need the quotient, so synthetic division is an efficient method.

Since $(x - 2)$ is a factor, the remainder is zero:

2	1	0	p	-2
		2	4	$2p + 8$
	1	2	$p + 4$	$2p + 6$ = 0 because $(x - 2)$ is a factor

$2p + 6 = 0$ so $p = -3$

Substituting for p, f(x) $= x^3 - 3x - 2$
       $= (x - 2)(x^2 + 2x + 1)$
       $= (x - 2)(x + 1)^2$

> **DON'T FORGET**
>
> Checking f(a) for various values of a likely to produce factors is best if you don't know any factors. However, if you are asked to verify a factor and also continue the factorisation, it makes sense to go straight to synthetic division, which does both things in one procedure.

> **DON'T FORGET**
>
> Always check when doing synthetic division for "missing" powers of x – you need to put 0 in the line of coefficients for any such term.

LET'S THINK ABOUT THIS

What more information would you want in order to make a rough sketch of the graph of the function in example 24, $y = x^3 - 3x - 2$?

GRAPHS OF POLYNOMIAL FUNCTIONS

CURVE SKETCHING FOR POLYNOMIAL FUNCTIONS

This is an extension of quadratic curve sketching. There's a bit more to it, though.

Example 25

Sketch the cubic function from example 24, $f(x) = x^3 - 3x - 2$.

Quite a bit of work has been done already (the factors tell us where the graph cuts the x-axis): $(x - 2)$ gives us $x = 2$, and $(x + 1)^2$ gives a double root at $x = -1$, which means there will be a stationary point there.

The next useful piece of information is the point of intersection with the y-axis.

Work it out: $x = 0$ so $y = -2$ $(0, -2)$

You could start drawing a rough sketch from the information found so far. Remember that the graph cannot cut the axes at any other points than those we have found so far.

To be a continuous line, there must be a turning point between $x = -1$ and $x = 2$. We need to differentiate f(x). We can also find out the shape for $x < -1$ using calculus, although it is much easier to find out if the graph is above or below the x-axis by evaluating, say, f(−2).

In fact, $f(2) = -4$, and so the graph is below the x-axis. Since we know there are no more roots, it must stay below.

$f'(x) = 3x^2 - 3 = 3(x^2 - 1) = 0$ for stationary points

Solving the equation, we find stationary points at $x = 1, -1$

$x = -1$ is no surprise, as we'd already deduced a stationary point there, but it's always reassuring when the next step backs up the step before. Calculating the value of f'(x) on either side of $x = -1$ provides evidence that (−1, 0) is a maximum turning point.

$x = 1 \Rightarrow f(1) = 1 - 3 - 2 = -4$ $(1, -4)$

Again, calculus should be used to verify that it's a minimum turning point.

This information fills in all the detail of the graph that you need.

Follow-up questions are sometimes asked about graphs of polynomial functions.

For example, for the cubic function in the last example:

what are the greatest and least values of f in the interval $0 \le x \le 3$?

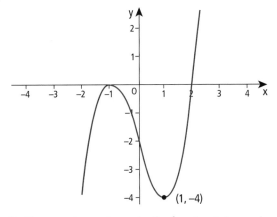

The least value can be seen to be −4 easily. However, beyond $x = 2$, the function is increasing (all the zeros and turning points have been found, so it can't do anything else), so we need to evaluate f(3): $f(3) = 3^3 - 3 \times 3 - 2 = 16$

The greatest and least values are 16 and −4.

FINDING APPROXIMATE ROOTS OF POLYNOMIAL FUNCTIONS

Of course, there are an infinite number of polynomial functions which don't conveniently pass through the x-axis at nice neat rational values like 2, –24, $\frac{1}{2}$. For a function that crosses the x-axis somewhere between $x = 2$ and $x = 3$, for example, we would use an **iterative** process to close in on the root.

Example 26

$x^3 + 2x^2 - 7 = 0$ has a root between 1 and 2. Find it correct to two decimal places.

Our method is to progressively narrow down the interval in which the root lies, by evaluating f(a) for sensibly chosen values of a between 1 and 2, as shown in the table.

	x	$f(x)$	root lies between
	1	–4	
	2	9	1 and 2
	1.5	0.875	1 and 1.5 looks much closer to 1.5
so try	1.4	–0.336	1.4 and 1.5
	1.45	0.2536	1.40 and 1.45
	1.43	0.140	1.40 and 1.43
	1.42	–0.1039 ...	1.42 and 1.43
	1.425	–0.045 ...	1.425 and 1.43 **so root is 1.43 to 2 dp**

> **DON'T FORGET**
>
> It is important always to work to one more decimal place than you will need in the answer. Then round off to the required number of decimal places at the last minute.

> **DON'T FORGET**
>
> You can calculate the value at the midpoint of the interval each time, or you can do a little guesswork on choosing the next value by looking at where you think it will cross. Play safe by using the midpoint unless you are really sure what you are doing.

FINDING POINTS OF INTERSECTION OF TWO CURVES

Two graphs of polynomial functions could have several points of intersection (or none at all). Where they exist, they can be found, just as we found points of intersection of a line and a parabola earlier.

Example 27

Find all the points of intersection of the curves $y = -x^3 + 12x + 4$
and $\qquad\qquad\qquad\qquad\qquad\qquad y = x^2 + 6x + 4$

Equate expressions for y: $x^2 + 6x + 4 = -x^3 + 12x + 4$
$$x^3 + x^2 - 6x = 0$$
$$x(x^2 + x - 6) = 0$$
$$x(x - 2)(x + 3) = 0$$
$$x = 0, \ x = 2, \ x = -3$$

Substituting these values into the equation of either curve to calculate the y-coordinates, the points of intersection are found to be $(-3, -5)$, $(0, 4)$ and $(2, 20)$.

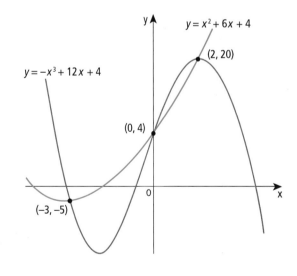

LET'S THINK ABOUT THIS

Another way to verify the shape of a polynomial graph at the extremities is to find whether y is large and positive or large and negative as x becomes very large positive or negative ($x \to \pm \infty$). Investigate this for the polynomial function in example 24 on p. 39, $y = x^3 - 3x - 2$.

EXPONENTIAL AND LOGARITHMIC FUNCTIONS

This is often seen as a difficult topic. The exponential function is met earlier, but not in much depth. Logs are not all that difficult to work with, but the topic comes near the end of the course – and, if time is tight, you might have not spent as much time getting comfortable at working with logs as you need. It's a steep learning curve! Make sure you find time to do enough practice examples from your textbook if you don't find enough here.

FUNCTIONS AND GRAPHS

INVERSE FUNCTIONS – GRAPHS AND FORMULAE

If the coordinates of the points on a graph are reversed (so that the inputs of the function become outputs and vice versa), and the new points plotted, the result is a graph of the inverse function. The graph of the inverse is the reflection of the original graph in the line $y = x$.

Notice the line of symmetry, $y = x$.

To see this symmetry, you need to have the same scale on both axes.

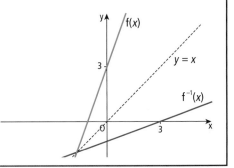

GRAPHS OF THE EXPONENTIAL AND LOGARITHMIC FUNCTIONS

The functions $f(x) = a^x$ and $f^{-1}(x) = \log_a x$ are inverses of each other.

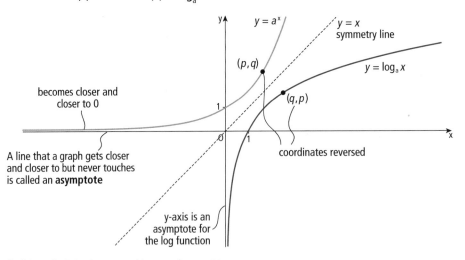

becomes closer and closer to 0

A line that a graph gets closer and closer to but never touches is called an **asymptote**

y-axis is an asymptote for the log function

coordinates reversed

"a" is called the **base**, and it must be positive.
For the graph to have the shape shown, a must be greater than 1.
(If $a = 1$, the graph collapses into a horizontal line passing through 1 on the y-axis.)

Different values of a will affect the steepness of the slope. However, the lines that the graphs approach but never touch, and the points (1, 0) and (0, 1), are unaffected by changes in the value of a.

contd

GRAPHS OF THE EXPONENTIAL AND LOGARITHMIC FUNCTIONS   contd

When $0 < a < 1$, something interesting happens. Do you remember what the graph of

$y = \left(\frac{1}{2}\right)^x$ looks like? Here is the algebra:

$y = \left(\frac{1}{2}\right)^x = \frac{1^x}{2^x} = \frac{1}{2^x} = 2^{-x}$

But the graph of $y = 2^{-x}$ is the reflection of $y = 2^x$ in the y-axis – remember the graph transformations on page 31. So, if $0 < a < 1$, the graph has this shape:

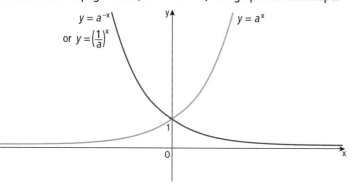

Taking a point on the exponential graph and its image on the logarithmic graph:

(p, q) lies on $y = a^x$ $\qquad\qquad$ (q, p) lies on $y = \log_a x$

Substituting in the coordinates: $q = a^p$ $\qquad$ $p = \log_a q$

The two statements above are equivalent – they are saying the same thing in different ways. You need to be expert in changing one to another.

Suppose $(125, 3)$ lay on the log graph. Then $3 = \log_a 125$

But $(3, 125)$ (point with coordinates reversed) must lie on the exponential graph $y = a^x$

so $125 = a^3$ (and $a = 5$ since $5^3 = 125$)

and so $\log_5 125 = 3$ the log equivalent of $5^3 = 125$

$y = \log_a x \iff x = a^y$

You are most likely not as good at thinking in logs as in powers, so you might find the following helpful.

To evaluate $\log_2 16$, you can think: "2 to what power gives 16?"

Since $2 \times 2 \times 2 \times 2 = 16$, the answer is 4.

If it's not an obvious easy one, for example $\log_5 \frac{1}{625}$ then call it, say, **p**, so that $p = \log_5 \frac{1}{625}$

Rewrite it as an exponential: $5^p = \frac{1}{625} = \frac{1}{5 \times 5 \times 5 \times 5} = 5^{-5}$

solving to give $p = -5$

Result: $\log_5 \frac{1}{625} = -5$

> **DON'T FORGET**
>
> $\log_2 8 = 3 \iff 2^3 = 8$
> $\log_a 5 = 4 \iff a^4 = 5$
> $\log_{10} 100\,000 = 5$
> $\qquad \iff 10^5 = 100\,000$
> Each line contains two equivalent statements – statements saying the same thing but in a diferent way.

> **DON'T FORGET**
>
> Very important!
> $a^0 = 1$
> $\log_a a = 1$
> $\log_a 1 = 0$
> These are true whatever the value of a.

LET'S THINK ABOUT THIS

Can you give a function which doesn't have an inverse, and say why it doesn't?

WORKING WITH EXPONENTIALS

USING YOUR CALCULATOR FOR EXPONENTIALS AND LOGS

Check you know the keys.

You should have a log key to work out logs to base 10, and the second function on this key is likely to be for calculating 10^x.

You should have a key LN which works out logs to base e, and its second function should calculate e^x. For each of these keys, you can "toggle" between the two functions to satisfy yourself that they are inverse functions.

An exponential to any base can be worked out using the "power" key, normally labelled x^y or $\wedge$. This is a key you were probably familiar with before beginning Higher Maths.

SIMPLE EVALUATIONS AND EQUATION-SOLVING WITH YOUR CALCULATOR

Examples of evaluations:

Using log and 10^x keys:

(1) $10^{3 \cdot 5} = 3162$ (2) $\log_{10} 45 = 1 \cdot 65$ (3) 10^{3t} where $t = 0 \cdot 04$ (4) $\log 5n$ where $n = 100$
                                                        $10^{0 \cdot 12} = 1 \cdot 32$ $\log 500 = 2 \cdot 70$

Using LN and e^x keys:

(1) $e^{3 \cdot 4} = 30 \cdot 0$ (2) $\log_e 589 = 6 \cdot 38$ (3) $e^{-0 \cdot 02t - 4}$ where $t = 40$ (4) $\ln (10k)$ where $k = 3 \cdot 7$
                                                        $e^{-4 \cdot 8} = 0 \cdot 00823$ $\ln 37 = 3 \cdot 61$

Examples of solving simple log and exponential equations, where the base is 10 or e, by rewriting log relationships as exponential ones:

(1) $\ln x = 8$ (2) $e^{3x} = 19$ (3) $10^{2y} = 4$ (4) $\log_{10} k = 2 \cdot 4$
    $x = e^8$ $3x = \ln 19$ $2y = \log_{10} 4$ $k = 10^{2 \cdot 4}$
    $x = 2980$ $3x = 2 \cdot 94$ $2y = 0 \cdot 60$ $k = 251$
                          $x = 0 \cdot 98$ $y = 0 \cdot 3$

EXPONENTIAL GROWTH AND DECAY

Problems involving exponentials in real-life situations of exponential growth, radioactive decay and so on come up in the exam regularly and are not very well done. The maths is just what we've looked at above, but the questions can seem complicated, which is presumably what puts people off tackling them sensibly.

contd

EXPONENTIAL GROWTH AND DECAY contd

The first part of most questions involves an evaluation of an exponential expression which might look rather complicated but doesn't involve any more maths than above.

Example 1

a The amount, A_t micrograms, of a particular radioactive substance remaining after t years decreases according to the formula $A_t = A_0 e^{-0.003t}$ where A_0 is the amount present initially.

If 250 micrograms are left after 500 years, how many micrograms were present initially?

From this, we have $A_t = 250$ $t = 500$ so we substitute them into the formula:

$A_t = A_0 e^{-0.003t}$

giving $250 = A_0 e^{-1.5}$

$A_0 = \dfrac{250}{e^{-1.5}}$ This is no problem to evaluate using the calculator

$= \textbf{1120 micrograms}$.

DON'T FORGET

Although it's more usual in exam questions to be given the initial value and asked the value after a given period of time (which is actually easier), you should be able to do this sort too.

The second part usually involves finding how long it takes for the value to go up or down a certain amount. In radioactivity questions it will be down, and often the half-life is involved – the time it takes for the amount of the radioactive substance to fall to half of its original amount.

Here's a second part of the example above:

b Find the half-life of the substance.

Rearranging the formula $e^{-0.003t} = \dfrac{A_t}{A_0} = 0.5$ (0.5, because A_t has to be half of A_0)

Now rewrite $e^{-0.003t} = 0.5$ in log form: $\ln 0.5 = -0.003t$

(evaluating $\dfrac{\ln 0.5}{-0.003}$) $t = 231$ **The half life is 231 years.**

DON'T FORGET

Usually you will be given values of A_0 and A_t to substitute, and unless it's a radioactivity question you will then have a different value for the ratio instead of 0.5, but there's no difference in how you work on from there.

Another type of question you could meet involves an exponent other than e or 10, making the technique "take logs of both sides" necessary. Here it is at work:

Example 2

The size, N, of a colony of bacteria after t hours is given by $N(t) = 640 \times (3.4)^{0.4t}$
Find the initial size of the colony and how long it takes for the size of the colony to be multiplied by 10.

Since $t = 0$ at the start, we are evaluating "something to the power zero", which is always 1, so $N(0) = 640$

Ten times that number is 6400, so the next part involves solving

$6400 = 640 \times (3.4)^{0.4t}$

$(3.4)^{0.4t} = 10$

Now we take logs of both sides – we'll use base 10, but e would work just as well:

$\log (3.4)^{0.4t} = \log 10$

$0.4t \log 3.4 = \log 10$ using $\log a^b = b \log a$ (the third law of logarithms on the next page)

$0.4t = \dfrac{\log 10}{\log 3.4}$ easily worked out with log key on calculator

$t = \dfrac{1.88}{0.4} = \textbf{4.7 hours}$

LET'S THINK ABOUT THIS

Why do you think, of all the possible numbers which could be used for bases for logarithms to be calculated, were 10 and e (2.718281 …) chosen?

WORKING WITH LOGARITHMS

THE LAWS OF LOGS

Never forget these rules for working with exponentials:

(1) $a^p \times a^q = a^{p+q}$ (2) $\frac{a^p}{a^q} = a^{p-q}$ (3) $(a^p)^q = a^{pq}$

Here are the three important logarithm laws derived from the above three rules which you must also learn and remember. They are true for all bases.

(1) $\log a + \log b = \log ab$ (2) $\log a - \log b = \log \frac{a}{b}$ (3) $\log x^n = n \log x$

So, for example:

$\log 4 + \log 5 = \log 20$ $\log 5 - \log 2 = \log \frac{5}{2}$ $\log 3^2 = 2 \log 3$

You can check that these examples are true for base 10 and base e with your calculator, should you still find they look strange.

Examples solving equations with logs: A/B

1 Solve $\log_3 (2x + 31) - \log_3 (x - 1) = 2$

$\log_3 \frac{2x + 31}{x - 1} = 2$ using the second law

$3^2 = \frac{2x + 31}{x - 1}$ rewriting as an exponential statement

$9x - 9 = 2x + 31$ and from here on it's easy:
$7x = 40$
$x = \frac{40}{7}$

2 The point $(a, 0)$ lies on the curve with equation $y = \log_4 (x + 3) - 3.6$. Find the value of a.

Finding points on graphs is often about substituting and solving, as here.

Substitute 0 and a: $0 = \log_4 (a + 3) - 3.6$
$\log_4 (a + 3) = 3.6$
$a + 3 = 4^{3.6}$ exponential turned into log
$a = 144$ using calculator

USING LOGS TO ESTABLISH FORMULAS SUCH AS $y = kx^n$ AND $y = ab^x$

Here you will be dealing with a straight-line graph where one or both of the axes are labelled $\log x$ or $\log y$ instead of x and y. In reality, this would be used for data from experiments, and the straight line is the best-fitting line through the data. You have to work out the equation of the straight line to find the missing constants in the formulas.

You need to see these graphs as very different from working with graphs of functions like $y = \log x$ as earlier in the chapter. Look at the labelling of the vertical axes – the relationship between x and y is more complicated.

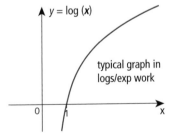

typical graph in logs/exp work

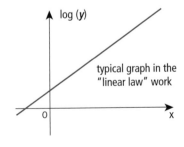

typical graph in the "linear law" work

contd

USING LOGS TO ESTABLISH FORMULAS SUCH AS $y = kx^n$ AND $y = ab^x$ contd

Example 1

x and y are related by the law $y = kx^n$ Find k and n.

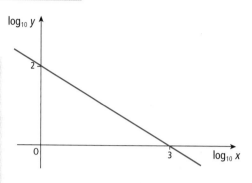

Working from the equation:

$$y = kx^n$$

$\log_{10} y = \log kx^n$
(taking logs of both sides)

$\log_{10} y = \log k + n \log_{10} x$
(using 1st and 3rd log law)

$\log_{10} y = n \log_{10} x + \log_{10} k$

Working from the graph:

y-intercept = 2

gradient $= -\frac{2}{3}$

equation: $\log_{10} y = -\frac{2}{3} \log_{10} x + 2$

(noticing the labels on the axes)

Since these two formulas represent the same relationship, we can equate the coefficients of the linear and constant term:

$n = -\frac{2}{3}$ $\log_{10} k = 2$

$k = 10^2 = 100$

the formula becomes $y = 100x^{-\frac{2}{3}}$

> **DON'T FORGET**
>
> log x and log y on the axes
> Linear law is
> $\qquad \log y = n \log x + \log k$
> Formula is $y = kx^n$

Example 2

The graph of $\log_{10} y$ against x has been drawn for some experimental data. It is known that the data fits an equation $y = ab^x$ for some constants a and b. Find the values of a and b.

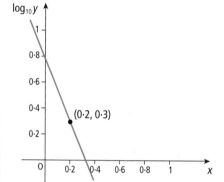

Working from equation:

$y = ab^x$

$\log_{10} y = \log ab^x$

$\log_{10} y = \log_{10} a + x \log b$

$\log_{10} y = (\log_{10} b) x + \log_{10} a$

Working from graph:

y-intercept = 0·8

gradient $= \frac{0·3 - 0·8}{0·2 - 0} = -2·5$

equation: $\log_{10} y = -2·5x + 0·8$

Equating coefficients: $\log_{10} b = -2·5 \Rightarrow b = 10^{-2·5}$

and: $\log_{10} a = 0·8 \Rightarrow a = 10^{0·8}$

and the formula is $y = 10^{-2·5} (10^{0·8x})$

> **DON'T FORGET**
>
> x and log y on the axes
> Linear law is
> $\qquad \log y = \log a + x \log b$
> Formula is $y = ab^x$

⚙ LET'S THINK ABOUT THIS

It is possible that you could be given a table of values instead of a graph – for example:

x	10	20	30	40	50
y	9·49	13·42	16·43	18·98	21·21

What would you do?

LOGARITHMIC AND EXPONENTIAL GRAPH TRANSFORMATIONS A/B

TRANSFORMATIONS OF THE EXPONENTIAL GRAPH

DON'T FORGET

If the alteration in the formula is to each appearance of "x", then the alteration to the graph will be a horizontal one. If it is to the whole expression for y, the change to the graph will be vertical.

Exponential graphs can be transformed in the same way as other graphs, and you can be given such a graph and asked to find its formula. We use the results from the section on Transformations of Graphs, (pages 30–31), applied to the graph of $y = e^x$.

Adding a constant to x moves the graph **horizontally**, and adding to the whole expression for y moves it **vertically**, so:

$y = a^{(x+1)}$ is the graph of $y = a^x$ moved 1 unit **left**, in the blue graph

$y = a^x + 1$ is the graph of $y = a^x$ moved **up** 1, the green graph.

A clue to this type would be the graph approaching the line $y = 1$ instead of the x-axis as $x \to \infty$.

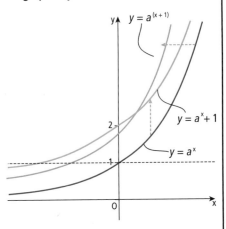

DON'T FORGET

Notice that it is by doing algebra on the exponential formulas, as in the examples here, that we can see what transformation has taken place.

But notice that $y = a^{(x+1)} = a^x \times a^1 = a(a^x)$. The effect of this is to multiply all the y-values on the graph of $y = a^x$ by a constant, a, which means the result is the graph of $y = a^x$ stretched vertically.

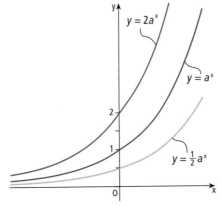

Multiplying by k stretches the graph vertically if $k > 1$ and compresses it if $k < 1$.

Notice that a stretch transformation alters the distance between the asymptote line and the point of intersection of the graph with the y-axis, so look out for that.

DON'T FORGET

Look out for hints for coordinates to substitute, for example where the graph cuts the y-axis so that $y = 0$, and also what line the graph gets closer and closer to.

$y = -a^x$ is the reflection of $y = a^x$ in the x-axis (so, a vertical-type transformation as you would expect).

$y = a^{-x}$ is the reflection in the y-axis, as we saw earlier in the chapter.

TRANSFORMATIONS OF THE LOGARITHMIC GRAPH

DON'T FORGET

A hint that the transformation is a $\log(x + k)$ type is that the graph will approach the line $x = k$ instead of the line $x = 0$ (the y-axis).

To be really on top of this topic, you need to be able to do the algebra of logs.

$y = \log x + k$ will be the graph of $\log x$ moved up k units (down if k is negative, of course), the pink graph.

$y = \log(x + k)$ is $y = \log x$ moved k to the left (or right if $k < 0$), the green graph

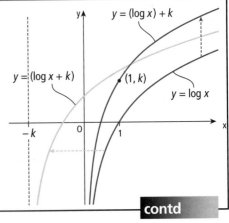

contd

TRANSFORMATIONS OF THE LOGARITHMIC GRAPH   contd

Example 1

Sketch the graph of $y = \log_3 81x$

$\log_3 81x = \log_3 81 + \log_3 x = \log_3 3^4 + \log_3 x = 4\log_3 3 + \log_3 x = 4 + \log_3 x$

which means $y = \log_3 81x$ is the graph of $y = \log_3 x$ moved up 4 units, which you certainly could be forgiven for not noticing (except you won't be forgiven in the exam!) – so watch out for this.

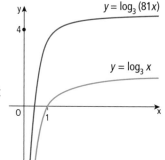

The graph of $y = k \log x$ will be the graph of $y = \log x$ stretched up and down by a factor of k.

Don't forget that, as $\log x^k = k \log x$, $y = \log x^k$ is just the same graph – in disguise.

The graph of $y = -\log x$ is the reflection of the graph of $y = \log x$ in the x-axis, as you would expect from knowing your transformations from Unit 1. But, again, some disguise might be involved:

$\log \frac{1}{x} = \log 1 - \log x = 0 - \log x$ so

$y = \log \frac{1}{x}$ is the same graph as $y = -\log x$.

If you are given a graph to identify, you will almost certainly be given clues as to the type of transformation (such as the form of the answer, $y = \log_a (x - b)$, for example).

Remember that a basic log graph gets close to but doesn't touch the y-axis and also passes through the point (1, 0). Look to see how these features have been moved – this will give you information.

You will also need to use the laws of logs.

Here is an example of a type which has caused trouble in exams in the past.

DON'T FORGET

Substituting the coordinates of any points marked on the graph into the equation of the graph can be very useful.

Example 2

The equation of the graph shown has formula $y = \log_b (x - a)$. Find a and b.

The graph certainly looks like the basic log graph moved to the right 3 units, which makes $a = 3$.

This can be verified by substituting the coordinates of the point (4, 0) into the formula:

$y = \log_b (4 - a) = 0$ and turning this into an exponential statement:
$b^0 = 4 - a$ (but $b^0 = 1$)
$a = 3$

Now, substituting the other point:
$\log_b (7 - a) = 2$
$\log_b 4 = 2$ (since $a = 3$)
And this gives $b^2 = 4$, so $b = 2$

The formula is $y = \log_2 (x - 3)$.

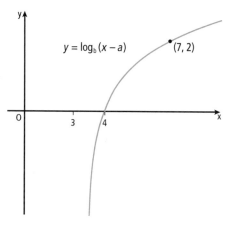

LET'S THINK ABOUT THIS

Can you do the algebra to show that the point of intersection of the two graphs $y = a^{(x+1)}$ and $y = a^x + 1$ has x-coordinate $\log_a \frac{1}{a-1}$?

Those who could do it in the 2003 Higher exam gained the final three marks in the whole paper, and usually the last marks in the exam are difficult marks to get.

Differentiation and integration are parts of calculus. There is some calculus in each of the units of Higher.

BASIC RULES OF DIFFERENTIATION

POWER RULE

Rule: If $f(x) = ax^n$ $f'(x) = anx^{n-1}$

"Multiply the coefficient by the power, and reduce the power by one."

Here are some examples, differentiating with respect to x, except in Example 1.13 which differentiates with respect to t.

1.1 $y = 5x^3$ **1.2** $f(x) = \frac{1}{2}x^9$ **1.3** $s = 6t^{\frac{1}{2}}$

$\quad \frac{dy}{dx} = 15x^2$ $f'(x) = 4\cdot 5x^8$ $\frac{ds}{dt} = 3t^{-\frac{1}{2}}$

Since $a = ax^0$, the derivative of a, or any constant, is 0.

Negative powers of x are dealt with no differently from positive.

1.4 $f(x) = 4x^{-2}$

$\quad f'(x) = -8x^{-3}$

1.5 $y = -x^{-\frac{5}{6}}$

$\quad \frac{dy}{dx} = \frac{5}{6}x^{-\frac{11}{6}}$ (since $-\frac{5}{6} - 1 = -\frac{5}{6} - \frac{6}{6} = -\frac{11}{6}$)

1.6 $y = 5p + 8$

$\quad \frac{dy}{dx} = 0$ (since there are no x-terms)

$\quad$ But notice, $\frac{dy}{dp} = 5$

Differentiating sums of powers of x is no problem – just differentiate each term in order:

1.7 $y = 6x + 4x^3 - x^{-2} - 3x^{-\frac{3}{2}} + 5$

$\quad \frac{dy}{dx} = 6 + 12x^2 + 2x^{-3} + \frac{9}{2}x^{-\frac{5}{2}}$

(in general, leave answers with fractions rather than decimals).

Rewrite roots as powers before differentiating:

1.8 To differentiate: $y = 4\sqrt{x} + 5\sqrt[3]{x} + 7\sqrt[3]{x^2}$ with respect to x

$\quad$ Rewrite as: $y = 4x^{\frac{1}{2}} + 5x^{\frac{1}{3}} + 7x^{\frac{2}{3}}$

$\quad\quad\quad\quad\quad \frac{dy}{dx} = 2x^{-\frac{1}{2}} + \frac{5}{3}x^{-\frac{2}{3}} + \frac{14}{3}x^{-\frac{1}{3}}$

Brackets need to be multiplied out first:

1.9 $f(x) = (x - 3)(x^2 + 5x - 8)$

$\quad\quad\quad = x^3 + 2x^2 - 23x + 24$

$\quad f'(x) = 3x^2 + 4x - 23$

Powers of x within fraction expressions need careful rewriting before differentiating:

1.10 $y = \frac{5}{x^3} = 5x^{-3}$

$\quad \frac{dy}{dx} = -15x^{-4}$

1.11 $f(x) = \frac{54x^5}{6x^2} = 9x^3$

$\quad f'(x) = 27x^2$

DON'T FORGET

Remember – the labels for the derivative need to match the question.

DON'T FORGET

Your basic arithmetic with fractions and negatives needs to be sound. Do lots of practice if necessary.

DON'T FORGET

"With respect to ..." tells you what to take as the variable for differentiating. Any other letters, standing for constants or variables, are treated as constants for the differentiation.

DON'T FORGET

There are different ways to work with fractions, as in examples 1.12 and 1.13 – use what you know best.

---

contd

POWER RULE contd

1.12 $\frac{d}{dx}\left(\frac{3x^5 + 2x^3 - 8x}{2\sqrt{x}}\right) = \frac{d}{dx}(\frac{3}{2}x^{\frac{9}{2}} + x^{\frac{5}{2}} - 4x^{\frac{1}{2}})$ (remember, $\sqrt{x} = x^{\frac{1}{2}}$ and you must divide each term by $2x^{\frac{1}{2}}$)

$$= \frac{27}{4}x^{\frac{7}{2}} + \frac{5}{2}x^{\frac{3}{2}} - 2x^{-\frac{1}{2}}$$

1.13 $f(x) = \frac{(x+4)(x-5)}{x^2}$

$$= \frac{x^2 - x - 20}{x^2}$$

$$= \frac{x^2}{x^2} - \frac{x}{x^2} - \frac{20}{x^2}$$

$$= 1 - x^{-1} - 20x^{-2}$$

The example is now in differentiable form – it is ready to be differentiated. Remember, in spite of all this work so far, you still haven't dfferentiated!

$$f'(x) = +x^{-2} + 40x^{-3}$$

1.14 $f(x) = 2\pi x^3$

π is a constant, so is treated like any other real number.

$$f'(x) = 6\pi x^2$$

> **DON'T FORGET**
>
> In these last two examples, the expression is rewritten as a sum of terms – a string of separate terms in x added/subtracted together. This must always be done before differentiating.

EVALUATING DERIVATIVES

You could be asked to "find $f'(3)$" or "find the rate of change of f at $x = 3$".

This involves substituting the value given into the expression for the derivative.

Example 2

For the equation $y = 3x^3 + 2x - \frac{4}{x} + 3$, find the rate of change at $x = -1$.

$$\frac{dy}{dx} = 9x^2 + 2 + 4x^{-2}$$

when $x = -1$, $\frac{dy}{dx} = 9 \times (-1)^2 + 2 + \frac{4}{(-1)^2}$

$$= 9 + 2 + 4$$

$$= 15$$

Example 3

Find $f'(x)$ when $x = 4$ for the formula for s in example 13.

$f'(x) = x^{-2} + 40x^{-3}$

$\quad\quad = \frac{1}{x^2} + \frac{40}{x^3}$

$f'(4) = \frac{1}{16} + \frac{40}{64}$

$\quad\quad = \frac{44}{64}$

$\quad\quad = \frac{11}{16}$

> **DON'T FORGET**
>
> You might want to rewrite it with negative powers of x transferred back to the denominator before substituting. Whatever way is reliable for you, use it.

 LET'S THINK ABOUT THIS

Differentiate $P = \frac{2r^2t^3}{s}$ with respect to r.

CALCULUS

COMPOSITE FUNCTIONS AND THEIR DIFFERENTIATION

You need to be able to establish formulae for composite functions. These are tested in Unit 1, and in the final exam, without involving any calculus. You also need to be able to break down a composite function into its parts in order to differentiate it.

 THE ALGEBRA OF COMPOSITE FUNCTIONS

$f(g(x))$ is a composite function formed from the two functions $f(x)$ and $g(x)$.

Example 4

Let $f(x) = x^2$ $g(x) = \cos x$ and $h(x) = 7 - x$

Then $f(g(x)) = (g(x))^2 = (\cos x)^2 = \cos^2 x$

$h(f(x)) = 7 - (f(x)) = 7 - (x^2) = 7 - x^2$

$g(f(x)) = g(x^2) = \cos(x^2)$

$h(h(x)) = 7 - h(x) = 7 - (7 - x) = x$

Notice that this last result shows that the function **h** happens to be its own inverse. This is not usual though.

Starting with an element in the domain, x, first the inner function acts on x, then the outer function works on the result. Untangling some composite functions (working backwards), where the functions f, g and h are the same as above:

$7 - \cos x = 7 - g(x) = h(g(x))$ **g** acts first on x, then **h** acts on the resulting expression.

$49 - 14x + x^2 = (7 - x)^2 = (h(x))^2 = f(h(x))$

Example 5

Solve the equation $f(h(x)) - 2h(f(x)) = 40$

First, substitute the expressions already worked out in Example 4:

$49 - 14x + x^2 - 2(7 - x^2) = 40$ a quadratic equation.

Simplify it:

$3x^2 - 14x - 5 = 0$ $(3x + 1)(x - 5) = 0$ $x = -\frac{1}{3}$ or $x = 5$

THE CHAIN RULE FOR DIFFERENTIATING COMPOSITE FUNCTIONS **Unit 3**

This is the method for dealing with a polynomial in x (which will be written inside a bracket), raised to a power. There are two ways of writing it out. Here is one.

Chain Rule $\frac{d}{dx}[(f(x))^n] = n[f(x)]^{n-1} \times f'(x)$

Fortunately, actual examples don't look as complicated as this suggests!

Follow the working in the examples below to make sure you remember how to do it.

Example 6

$f'(x) = (x + 6)^{-3}$ $y = \sqrt{x - 5}$
$f'(x) = -3(x + 6)^{-2}$ $= (x - 5)^{\frac{1}{2}}$

$\frac{dy}{dx} = \frac{1}{2}(x - 5)^{\frac{1}{2}}$

$= \frac{1}{2\sqrt{x - 5}}$

The chain rule for differentiating composite functions contd

Example 7 A/B

Differentiate $y = (3x + 5)^4$ with respect to x.

Looking at the form it's in, we have $y = (f(x))^4$ contributing $4(f(x))^3$ to the answer. We also need to include the derivative of f(x), the expression in the bracket: $f'(x) = 3$

Putting it together: $\frac{dy}{dx} = 4(3x + 5)^3 \times 3 = 12(3x + 5)^3$

Example 8 A/B

Find $\frac{dy}{dx}$ if $y = \sqrt{5x^2 + 3x - 7}$

We need to rewrite: $y = (5x^2 + 3x - 7)^{-\frac{1}{2}}$ to see that we have a similar form to the previous example.

Now use the chain rule:

$\frac{dy}{dx} = \frac{1}{2}(5x^2 + 3x - 7)^{-\frac{1}{2}} \times (10x + 3) = \frac{10x + 3}{2\sqrt{5x^2 + 3x - 7}}$

Example 9 A/B

Differentiate $f(x) = \frac{3}{(5x - 2)^4}$

First, rewrite as $f(x) = 3(5x - 2)^{-4}$

$f'(x) = -12(5x - 2)^{-5} \times 5 = -60(5x - 2)^{-5} = \frac{-60}{(5x - 2)^5}$

DON'T FORGET

If the example is an expression raised to power 2 (or even 3), such as $(2x + 3)^2$, it could be just as quick to multiply it out – the choice is yours.

DON'T FORGET

Try to leave your answers with positive indices and simplified as much as you can.

ALTERNATIVE METHOD FOR NOTATING THE CHAIN RULE   Unit 3

Chain rule: $\frac{dy}{dx} = \frac{dy}{du} \times \frac{du}{dx}$

To work the example above this way, we would write:

$u = 5x^2 + 3x - 7$ so that $y = (5x^2 + 3x - 7)^{\frac{1}{2}} = u^{\frac{1}{2}}$

$\frac{dy}{du} = \frac{1}{2}u^{-\frac{1}{2}}$

This will mean also that $\frac{du}{dx} = 10x + 3$
(differentiating u with respect to x)

Now we can substitute these expressions in $\frac{dy}{dx} = \frac{dy}{du} \times \frac{du}{dx}$

obtaining $\frac{dy}{dx} = \frac{1}{2}u^{-\frac{1}{2}} \times (10x + 3)$

but we need to substitute for u to complete it:

$= \frac{1}{2}(5x^2 + 3x - 7)^{-\frac{1}{2}} (10x + 3)$

as obtained earlier.

To use the chain rule, you really have to see the structure of it clearly, but if you fully understand you will probably find it easy to use, especially for the more complex examples which you will meet if you take Maths beyond Higher.

LET'S THINK ABOUT THIS

Work out example 9 using the alternative method.

BASIC RULES OF INTEGRATION

INTEGRATION – ANTI-DIFFERENTIATION

Apart from one complicating feature – more of that in a moment – if you integrate the result of a differentiation, you should get the original expression back. And vice versa: if you differentiate the result of an integration, you end up with the original expression.

The integral of $f(x)$ is written $\int f(x)dx$

Don't forget the "dx"!

Here's a diagram to remind you of a term which is a power of x:

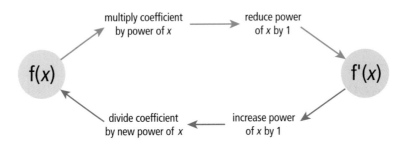

For example, to integrate the term $4x^3$ increase the power by 1 $\ x^4$

divide coefficient by new power $\frac{4}{4} = 1$ so the answer is $\ x^4$

And, for this term, $\frac{6}{x^3}$, first rewrite as $6x^{-3}$

increase the power by 1 $\ x^{-2}$

divide coefficient by new power $\frac{6}{-2} = -3$ so the answer is $-\frac{3}{x^3}$

So much for integrating individual terms in a polynomial expression. The complicating feature mentioned above is constant terms. The following three expressions are the same except for the constant terms:

$$\left.\begin{array}{l}3x^2 - 5x + 4 \\ 3x^2 - 5x - 7 \\ 3x^2 - 5x\end{array}\right\}\ \text{all differentiate to give } 6x - 5$$

Integrating $6x - 5$ gives the terms $3x^2 - 5x$ and it is impossible to know without further information what the constant term could be. So, we write C (C is the usual letter used anyway) to indicate the presence of a constant in the anti-derivative (which could of course be zero). So, $\int(6x - 5)dx = 3x^2 + 5x + C$ and, unless there is information to enable you to find C (which in the exam there usually is), that is how you should write the answer.

Integration Rule

$\int kx^n dx = k\int x^n dx = \frac{kx^{n+1}}{n+1} + C$ provided $n \neq -1$

contd

DON'T FORGET

Particularly in Unit tests, not mentioning the constant will lose you a whole mark.

DON'T FORGET

"provided $n \neq -1$" means you cannot calculate $\int \frac{1}{x}dx$

INTEGRATION – ANTI-DIFFERENTIATION contd

Examples

10 Integrate $\frac{7}{x^2}$ with respect to x.

Rewrite $\frac{7}{x^2}$ as $7x^{-2}$ $\int 7x^{-2}dx = \frac{7x^{-1}}{-1} + C = -\frac{7}{x} + C$

11 Find $\int p(2p + 1)(p - 6)dp$

Brackets must be multiplied out first: $\int p(2p + 1)(p - 6)dp = \int (2p^3 - 11p^2 - 6p)dp$

$= \frac{2p^4}{4} - \frac{11p^3}{3} - \frac{6p^2}{2} + C$

$= \frac{1}{2}p^4 - \frac{11}{3}p^3 - 3p^2 + C$

12 Find $\int (3ps + qs^2)ds$

"ds" tells us that s is the variable which we are integrating with respect to, and so p and q are constants (for the purposes of the integration, at least).

$\int (3ps + qs^2)ds =$
$\frac{3ps^2}{2} + \frac{qs^3}{3} + C$

There is another important type of example which is all about checking that you understand that differentiation and integration are inverse processes:

13 a Differentiate $\sqrt{x^4 + 8}$

  b Hence write down $\int \frac{x^3 dx}{\sqrt{x^4 + 8}}$

Differentiating for **a**:

$\frac{d}{dx}(x^4 + 8)^{\frac{1}{2}} = \frac{1}{2}(x^4 + 8)^{-\frac{1}{2}} \times 4x^3 = \frac{2x^3}{\sqrt{x^4 + 8}}$

Now **b**:

Reversing the process, we can see that, as $\int \frac{2x^3 dx}{\sqrt{x^4 + 8}} = \sqrt{x^4 + 8}$,

$\int \frac{x^3 dx}{\sqrt{x^4 + 8}} = \frac{1}{2}\sqrt{x^4 + 8} + C$

DON'T FORGET

You can be asked to differentiate and integrate with respect to different variables. Only one at a time though – see example 3.

DON'T FORGET

"Hence" always means following on from the earlier part of the question, so there is a huge clue there.

INTEGRATING $(ax + b)^n$ Unit 3

There is no "chain rule" equivalent for integration, but the formula here is useful:

Rule $\int (ax + b)^n dx = \frac{(ax + b)^{n+1}}{a(n + 1)} + C$ (provided $a \neq 0$, and $n \neq -1$)

Example 14

Integrate $\frac{-60}{(5x - 2)^5}$ with respect to x.

First, rewrite as $-60(5x - 2)^{-5}$

Compare with $(ax + b)^n$ $a = 5$, $n = -5$

$\int -60(5x - 2)^{-5}dx = \frac{-60(5x - 2)^{-4}}{5x - 4} + C = \frac{3}{(5x - 2)^4} + C$

You can see that this integration has reversed the differentiation at the end of the previous section.

DON'T FORGET

You can see the similarity with integrating powers of x, which is just as well, since this formula is not given in the formula list on the exam paper, so you must remember it.

 LET'S THINK ABOUT THIS

In the rule given above, why is $a = 0$, or $n = -1$, excluded? What happens if they aren't excluded?

DIFFERENTIATION AND INTEGRATION OF TRIGONOMETRIC FUNCTIONS Unit 3

DIFFERENTIATING AND INTEGRATING sin x AND cos x

$$\frac{d}{dx}(\sin x) = \cos x \qquad \frac{d}{dx}(\cos x) = -\sin x$$

A straightforward example is $y = 3 \sin x + 4 \cos x - 5x$

where differentiating gives $\frac{dy}{dx} = 3 \cos x - 4 \sin x - 5$

Since integrating is the inverse process, $\int \cos x \, dx = \sin x + C$

and $\int \sin x \, dx = -\cos x + C$

For example, $\int 3 \cos x + 5 \sin x + 3x^2 \, dx$
$$= 3 \sin x - 5 \cos x + x^3 + C$$

This diagram helps you remember how to get the correct term:

DON'T FORGET

Remember that each term is differentiated or integrated quite separately from the others.

sin x

cos x

−sin x

−cos x

differentiate   sin x   integrate

cos x

−sin x

etc.

USING THE CHAIN RULE TO DIFFERENTIATE TRIG FUNCTIONS

First, we can apply the chain rule in examples like sin ( ) or cos ( ) where the bracket contains a polynomial expression in x.

Example 15

Differentiate $\cos (3x)$ with respect to x.

Differentiating "cos" gives "−sin", so we start with −sin 3x.

Multiplying this by the derivative of $(3x)$, which is 3, the complete answer is:

−3 sin $(3x)$.

Example 16

Differentiate $y = \sin (4x + \pi)$

Differentiating "sin" gives "cos", so we have $\cos(4x + \pi)$ and we multiply by the derivative of the expression in the bracket, which is 4, so:

$$\frac{dy}{dx} = 4 \cos (4x + \pi)$$

DON'T FORGET

In the exam, it is likely that 3x will be inside brackets, though it is not necessary to write it like that, and your textbook and teacher probably don't. It is done in the exam to make sure there can be no ambiguity – don't let "extra" brackets put you off.

DON'T FORGET

π is a constant, so is treated like any other real number.

contd

USING THE CHAIN RULE TO DIFFERENTIATE TRIG FUNCTIONS contd

We can also apply the chain rule to functions which are powers of (sin x) rather than powers of x.

Example 17

$y = \sin^4 x = (\sin x)^4$

It is often clearer to rewrite powers of trig functions like this.

$\frac{d}{dx}[(f(x))^n] = n[f(x)]^{n-1} \times f'(x)$

$f(x) = \sin x$ so $f'(x) = \cos x$ $n = 4$

$\frac{dy}{dx} = 4(\sin x)^3 \times \cos x = 4\sin^3 x \cos x$

Here is an example worked out using the other way of working the chain rule:

$\frac{dy}{dx} = \frac{dy}{du} \times \frac{du}{dx}$

> **DON'T FORGET**
>
> Angles must always be in radians for this topic – not degrees.

Example 18

Differentiate $y = \sin \sqrt{x}$

Let $u = \sqrt{x} = \frac{1}{2}x^{-\frac{1}{2}}$ so $\frac{du}{dx} = \frac{1}{2}x^{-\frac{1}{2}}$

$\quad y = \sin u$ so $\frac{dy}{du} = \cos u$

$\frac{dy}{dx} = \frac{dy}{du} \times \frac{du}{dx} = \cos u \times \frac{1}{2}x^{-\frac{1}{2}} = \cos \sqrt{x} \times \frac{1}{2}x^{-\frac{1}{2}} = \frac{\cos \sqrt{x}}{2\sqrt{x}}$

Example 19

Find $\frac{dy}{dx}$ if $y = (3\cos(x) - 2)^4$

Using the substitution method:

Let $u = 3\cos(x) - 2$ so that

$\frac{du}{dx} = -3\sin(x)$ and $y = u^4$

$\frac{dy}{dx} = \frac{dy}{du} \times \frac{du}{dx}$

$\quad = 4u^3 \times -3\sin(x)$

$\quad = 4(3\cos(x) - 2)^3 \times -3\sin(x)$

$\quad = -12\sin(x)(3\cos(x) - 2)^3$

Alternatively, $y = (3\cos(x) - 2)^4$

$\frac{dy}{dx} = 4(3\cos(x) - 2)^3 \times \frac{d}{dx}(3\cos(x) - 2)$

$\quad = 4(3\cos(x) - 2)^3(-3\sin(x))$

$\quad = -12\sin(x)(3\cos(x) - 2)^3$

INTEGRATING sin ($ax + b$) AND cos ($ax + b$) A/B

Working backwards from differentiation, we have the rules:

$\int \sin(ax + b)dx = -\frac{1}{a}\cos(ax + b) + C$

$\int \cos(ax + b)dx = \frac{1}{a}\sin(ax + b) + C$

You can differentiate the right-hand sides in these rules to check that you obtain the left-hand sides.

> **DON'T FORGET**
>
> These rules for integration are given in the formula list at the beginning of the exam paper.

Example 20

Integrate $\cos(3x - 1)$ with respect to x.

Since $a = 3$, the answer will be $\frac{1}{3}\sin(3x - 1) + C$

Example 21

Find $\int \sin(\pi - 2x)dx$

$a = -2$ and $b = \pi$

$\int \sin(\pi - 2x)dx = \frac{1}{2}\cos(\pi - 2x) + C$

> **DON'T FORGET**
>
> To include "+ C" when integrating.

LET'S THINK ABOUT THIS

Differentiate $\sqrt{\sin x}$ and compare the answer with the derivative of $\sin \sqrt{x}$ from above.

DIFFERENTIATION – GRADIENTS

THE DERIVATIVE – GRADIENT

The graph of a cubic equation $y = x^3 - 12x - 4$ is shown in the diagram.

Straight lines have constant gradients, but the gradient of a curve varies as you move along it.

The gradient, $\frac{dy}{dx}$, gives the slope of the curve.

For $y = -3x + 5$ $\frac{dy}{dx} = -3$

So the slope of the derivative of $y = x^3 - 12x - 4$ is given by $\frac{dy}{dx} = 3x^2 - 12$

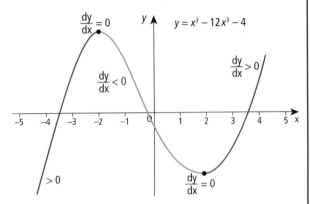

$\frac{dy}{dx}$ gives the numerical value of the gradient at any point on the curve – substitute the appropriate value of x into the formula for $\frac{dy}{dx}$

It can be seen from the diagram that the curve has zero gradient when $x = 2$ and $x = -2$.

This can be verified algebraically by calculating $\frac{dy}{dx}$ when $x = 2$, or -2, for example:

$\frac{dy}{dx} = 3x^2 - 12 = 3 \times 2^2 - 12 = 12 - 12 = 0$

The function is neither increasing nor decreasing at those values. It is said to be stationary.

$\frac{dy}{dx} = 0$ for stationary points.

When $-2 < x < 2$
the function is decreasing
the gradient is negative
the curve has a downward slope

$\frac{dy}{dx} < 0$

When $x < -2$ and $x > 2$
the function is increasing
the gradient is positive
the curve has an upward slope

$\frac{dy}{dx} > 0$

SKETCHING THE GRAPH OF THE DERIVATIVE

For the graph of $y = f(x)$, where $f(x) = x^3 - 12x - 4$ above, a table has been made up giving the gradient for different values of x. Check that you agree by comparing the graph and the table.

x	−3	−2	−1	0	1	2	3	...
$\frac{dy}{dx}$	+ve	0	−ve	−ve	−ve	0	+ve	

A graph plotting these positive, negative and zero values is shown below – the graph of the derived function, $y = f'(x)$.

As the gradient changes smoothly, never abruptly, the graph is continuous.

Notice that we do not need the exact values to obtain the overall shape.

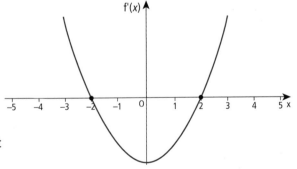

DON'T FORGET

The overall shape is what is required. If a particular value, such as the intersection with the y-axis, is wanted, the question should make it clear.

FINDING THE EQUATION OF A CURVE FROM THE DERIVATIVE

We can reverse the process above to find the equation of a curve from its gradient formula:

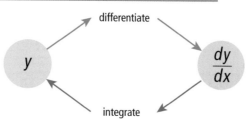

differentiate

integrate

DON'T FORGET

$\frac{dy}{dx} = 2x + 5$

is called a differential equation, as it contains a derivative.

Example 22

Find the equation of the curve $y = f(x)$ for which $\frac{dy}{dx} = 2x + 5$ and which passes through the point (0, 4).

By integrating, we can find a family of curves which have this gradient formula:

$y = x^2 + 5x + C$ is the equation for this family.

Different values of C give a set of curves which appear "parallel" to each other:

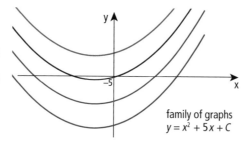

family of graphs
$y = x^2 + 5x + C$

DON'T FORGET

To find C so that you have the equation of one unique curve, you need a point on the curve to substitute, as in the working shown. Make sure you look in the question or diagram for this point.

Substituting the point (0, 4) into the equation:
$y = x^2 + 5x + C$

we have $4 = 0^2 + 5 \times 0 + C \Rightarrow C = 4$
so, the parabola has equation $y = x^2 + 5x + 4$ (blue curve on diagram)

Example 23

The graph shows a cubic function (in red) $y = f(x)$ and its derived function $y = f'(x)$ (in green).

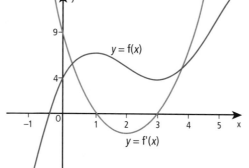

$y = f(x)$

$y = f'(x)$

a Use the points of intersection of the graph of $f'(x)$ with the axes to find the equation of the derived function.

b Find the equation of $f(x)$.

a The graph of $f'(x)$ cuts the x-axis at $x = 1$ and $x = 3$

$f'(x)$ has factors $(x - 1)$ and $(x - 3)$

$f'(x) = k(x-1)(x-3)$.

Expanding the brackets and substituting the point (0, 9):

$f'(x) = 3x^2 - 12x + 9$ (check this for yourself).

b $f(x) = \int f'(x)dx = \int (3x^2 - 12x + 9)\ dx = x^3 - 6x^2 + 9x + C$

and, since $f(x)$ passes through (0, 4), $C = 4$

$f(x) = x^3 - 6x^2 + 9x + 4$

DON'T FORGET

Any cubic function will have a quadratic function (that is, a parabola) for its derived function. Remembering that a parabola has a vertical axis of symmetry will help you sketch the derived function for a cubic equation.

DON'T FORGET

Always check the diagram for helpful information on points on the graph.

LET'S THINK ABOUT THIS

The derived function of a cubic is a quadratic. In general, what is the highest power of the derived function compared to the function, and what does this mean in terms of the shape of the derived and original function?

DIFFERENTIATION – EQUATIONS OF CURVES AND TANGENTS

INCREASING AND DECREASING FUNCTIONS

We can use $\frac{dy}{dx}$ to establish whether a function is increasing, decreasing or stationary at any point. The graph $y = x^3 - 12x - 4$ already discussed (shown on p. 58) increases and decreases, and it is stationary momentarily where it changes from one to the other.

Particularly interesting are questions like this:

Example 24

Show that the function $y = \frac{1}{3}x^3 + 3x^2 + 11x + 4$ is always increasing.

It's necessary to find $\frac{dy}{dx}$ and then show that it must be positive, whatever the value of x.

$$\frac{dy}{dx} = x^2 + 6x + 11$$
$$= (x^2 + 6x + 9) + 2$$
$$= (x + 3)^2 + 2 > 0 \text{ for all } x, \text{ so } y \text{ always increases.}$$

Example 24.1

For which values of x is the function $y = 6 + 5x + 2x^2 - \frac{1}{3}x^3$ decreasing?

$$\frac{dy}{dx} = 5 + 4x - x^2 = (5 - x)(1 + x) = 0 \quad x = -1, 5$$

Choosing a value of x between -1 and 5 and calculating $\frac{dy}{dx}$ at that point (for example, $x = 0$ gives $\frac{dy}{dx} = 5$) results in the graph of the derivative being the shape shown in the sketch.

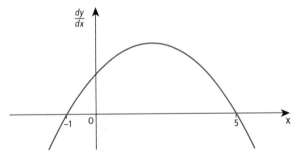

(You might prefer to think "∩-shaped parabola" and work out the shape as in "Solving quadratic inequations" on p. 35.)

The function is decreasing when $\frac{dy}{dx} < 0$, which is when $x < -1$ and when $x > 5$.

Example 25

Show that the function $f(x) = \sin(x) + x$ is never decreasing.
Is f(x) always increasing?

$f'(x) = \cos(x) + 1$

$-1 \le \cos x \le 1$ for all x

so $0 \le \cos(x) + 1 \le 2$ for all x

As $f'(x) \ge 0$ for all x, f(x) is never decreasing, but since $f'(x)$ can be equal to zero, the function can be stationary, so it is not always increasing.

EQUATIONS OF TANGENTS TO CURVES

Two tangents to the curve $y = x^3 - 12x - 4$ have been drawn, at $x = -3$ and $x = 1$.

$x = -3 \Rightarrow y = (-3)^3 - 12 \times (-3) - 4 = 5$

and $\frac{dy}{dx} = 3 \times (-3)^2 - 12 = 15$

so, at $(-3, 5)$ the gradient is 15.

Using $y - b = m(x - a)$, the equation of the tangent is $y - 5 = 15(x + 3) \Rightarrow y = 15x + 50$

$x = 1 \Rightarrow y = 1^3 - 12 \times 1 - 4 = -15$

and $\frac{dy}{dx} = 3 \times 1^2 - 12 = -9$

so, at $(1, -15)$ the gradient is –9 and the equation of the tangent is $y = -9x - 6$.

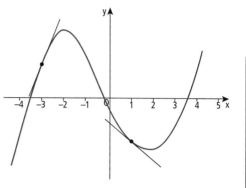

Example 26

Find the equation of the tangent at A, where $x = 4$, on the graph of $y = \frac{3}{\sqrt{x}}$, $x > 0$

$y = 3x^{-\frac{1}{2}}$

$\frac{dy}{dx} = 3(-\frac{1}{2}x^{-\frac{3}{2}}) = \frac{-3}{2x^{\frac{3}{2}}} = \frac{-3}{2\sqrt{x^3}} = \frac{3}{4}$

At $x = 4$ $m = \frac{-3}{2\sqrt{4^3}} = \frac{-3}{16}$

and $y = \frac{3}{\sqrt{4}} = \frac{3}{2}$

Substituting these into

$y - y_1 = m(x - x_1)$ and simplifying:

$y - \frac{3}{2} = -\frac{3}{16}(x - 4)$ $16y - 24 = -3x + 12$ **$16y + 3x = 36$**

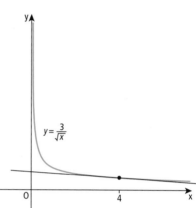

Example 27

The point Q lies on the curve with equation $y = x^3 - 3x^2$.

The tangent at Q has gradient –3. Find the equation of the tangent at Q.

$\frac{dy}{dx} = 3x^2 - 6x = -3$

Factorise and solve for x: $3(x^2 - 2x + 1) = 0 \Rightarrow (x - 1)^2 = 0$

$\Rightarrow x = 1$

When $x = 1$, $y = -2$

substituting into $y - y_1 = m(x - x_1)$ gives **$y = 3x + 1$**

Example 28

Find the equation of the tangent to the curve $y = 2 + \sin x$ at the point where $x = \pi$.

$\frac{dy}{dx} = \cos x$ when $x = \pi$ $y = 2 + \sin \pi = 2$

and $\frac{dy}{dx} = \cos \pi = -1$

substituting into $y - y = m(x - y)$
$y - 2 = -1(x - \pi)$
$y - 2 = -x + \pi$
$y + x = \pi + 2$

LET'S THINK ABOUT THIS

Draw graphs of two functions to show the difference between "never decreasing" and "always increasing".

DIFFERENTIATION – CURVE-SKETCHING

STATIONARY POINTS

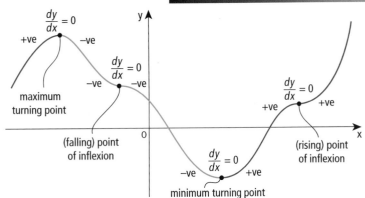

Particularly interesting on the graphs you might have to sketch or interpret are the points where the gradient of the tangent is zero.

These are the stationary points of the curve ("stationary" means that the curve is neither rising nor falling at that moment).

A stationary point can be

a a maximum or minimum turning point

b a rising or falling point of inflexion.

Not all points of inflexion are stationary points, however. This one, for example, isn't – the gradient *never* becomes zero. But you won't study these until Advanced Higher!

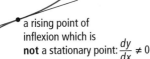

a rising point of inflexion which is **not** a stationary point: $\frac{dy}{dx} \neq 0$

Which of these four options is the correct one depends on the gradient (value of $\frac{dy}{dx}$) on either side of the stationary point. In the diagram, signs for positive and negative gradients have been entered on either side of the stationary points. Make sure you understand how the different combinations of positive and negative give the four possibilities.

Example 29

Find all the stationary points on the curve $y = x^4 - 2x^3$ and determine their nature.

$\frac{dy}{dx} = 4x^3 - 6x^2 = 0$ for stationary points

$2x^2(2x - 3) = 0 \Rightarrow x = 0, x = \frac{3}{2}$

Find the *y*-coordinates of the points $x = 0 \Rightarrow y = 0$ (0, 0)

$x = 1 \cdot 5 \Rightarrow y = -1 \cdot 69$ (2 dp) (1·5, −1·69)

Find the nature of each turning point by finding the gradient on each side, entering the information into a "nature table":

x	−0·1	0	0·1	…	1·4	1·5	1·6
$\frac{dy}{dx}$	−0·064	0	−0·056		−0·784	0	1·024
slope	\	—	\		\	—	/

The table shows that there is a (falling) point of inflexion at (0, 0) and a minimum turning point at (1·5, −1·69).

If a graphic calculator is available, this could be found out by graphing the function. Using the graphic calculator to verify a sketch is very reassuring, of course.

DON'T FORGET

Questions on curve-sketching could be in either paper, but in the non-calculator paper it should be possible to do appropriate working without requiring fraction or decimal calculations.

DON'T FORGET

If you have been taught to use the second derivative to investigate stationary points and are quite confident, even with points of inflexion, it is of course fine to use it.

CURVE-SKETCHING

It is not often that you are asked to sketch a function from just the formula. More often, a rough sketch will be given and you'll be asked to fill in some details, for example the coordinates of a stationary point, or an intersection with one of the axes so that a better sketch could be drawn. Where you are asked to sketch a graph, the question will usually be broken down into several parts. This will lead you through the steps needed to find all the important points to mark on your graph.

contd

CURVE-SKETCHING   contd

Example 30

Sketch the curve with equation $y = x^4 - 2x^3$

We have already done a large part of the work in the example above. In an exam, that might have been part (a) and the question here part (b).

In order to collect the information to sketch the curve, we do three things:

1   Find the stationary points and their nature
2   Find the points of intersection with the axes
3   Investigate the behaviour of the curve for large positive and negative x.

1   has already been done.

2   Find y-intercept: $x = 0$ gives $(0, 0)$
      x-intercept: $y = 0$
          $x^4 - 2x^3 = 0$
        $x^3(x - 2) = 0$
             $x = 0, 2$
giving $(0, 0)$ and $(2, 0)$
The only new information to come out of that is the point $(2, 0)$, but it is always reassuring to find this backing up what we already have.

3   Only the largest power of x determines whether the curve is positive or negative at the extremities, so here we look at the sign of x^4. Even powers will be positive, whether x is positive or negative, so,

as $x \to +\infty$, $y \to +\infty$
and as $x \to -\infty$, $y \to +\infty$

Putting all the information gathered onto a graph:

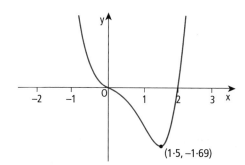

$(1 \cdot 5, -1 \cdot 69)$

> **DON'T FORGET**
>
> Odd powers alternate between positive and negative. Check these out:
>
> as $x \to +\infty$, $x^3 \to +\infty$
> but $-x^3 \to -\infty$
>
> and as $x \to -\infty$, $x^3 \to -\infty$
> and $-x^3 \to +\infty$

MAXIMUM AND/OR MINIMUM VALUE OF A FUNCTION ON A CLOSED INTERVAL

Example 31

What are the maximum and minimum values of $y = x^3 - 12x - 4$ within the interval $0 \le x \le 4$?

Look back at the graph of this function, on p. 58. If the vertical line $x = 4$ were drawn in, we would look for the highest and lowest value of y between the y-axis and the line $x = 4$, including on those lines. It looks as if the lowest value is at the minimum turning point and the highest on the line $x = 4$.

I'm sure you can see that maximum/minimum values will always occur at end points of the interval or at turning points, so turning points will need to be found if they haven't already.

$x = 0 \Rightarrow y = -4$ $x = 4 \Rightarrow y = 4^3 - 12 \times 4 - 4 = \mathbf{12}$

Turning point: $x = 2$ (from earlier example) and $y = 2^3 - 12 \times 2 - 4 = \mathbf{-20}$

so the **maximum value is 12** (when $x = 4$) and the **minimum value is –20** (when $x = 2$).

> **DON'T FORGET**
>
> There is no need to draw a nature table when finding maximum/minimum values on a closed interval.

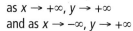 LET'S THINK ABOUT THIS

Why does the largest power of x in a polynomial determine the behaviour of the curve for large positive and negative x?

CALCULUS

PROBLEM-SOLVING USING DIFFERENTIATION

THE DERIVATIVE AS THE RATE OF CHANGE

$f'(x)$ or $\frac{dy}{dx}$ measures the rate of change, but so far we have used rate of change in the context of gradients and curves and discussed the situation from a geometric point of view.

There are other contexts where the jargon might be different but the same processes of calculus are used.

Example 32

Find the rate of change of the function $g(x) = 2x^2 - 12\sqrt{x}$ when $x = 3$.

The rate of change is $g'(x)$. If $x = 3$, we need to calculate $g'(3)$.

$g(x) = 2x^2 - x^{\frac{1}{2}}$

$g'(x) = 4x - \frac{1}{2}x^{-\frac{1}{2}}$ and so $g'(3) = 12 - \dfrac{1}{2\sqrt{3}}$

Example 33

A balloon is attached to a pump and is expanding so that its diameter in cm after t seconds is given by the formula $d(t) = 18\sqrt[3]{t}$. What is the rate of change of the diameter after 8 seconds?

$d(t) = 18t^{\frac{1}{3}}$ Rate of change is $d'(t) = 6t^{-\frac{2}{3}}$

For the rate of change after 8 seconds, calculate $d'(8)$:

$d'(8) = \dfrac{6}{\sqrt[3]{64}} = \dfrac{6}{4} = \mathbf{1{\cdot}5 \text{ cm per second}}$.

That's the answer, but of course you can solve problems much better if you know what they're all about. The rate of change tells us that the balloon's diameter is increasing with respect to t at 1·5 cm/sec after 8 seconds, but this is only true for a moment. Common sense tells us that the diameter increases fast when the balloon starts being blown up and more slowly as time passes. After 8 seconds, the balloon's diameter is 36 cm, and increasing slowly.

Example 34

The current in an electrical circuit is given by the formula $I(R) = \frac{250}{R}$ amps where R is the resistance measured in ohms. When the resistance is 15 ohms, what is the rate of change of the current, I?

$I(R) = 250R^{-1}$
$\Rightarrow I'(R) = -250R^{-2}$

$R = 15$ so calculate $I'(15) = -250 \times \frac{1}{15^2} = -\frac{250}{225} = \mathbf{-1{\cdot}11 \text{ amps/ohm}}$.

Example 35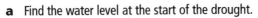

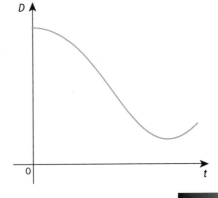

An example of rate of change where trigonometry is used:

The water level in a reservoir during a month of drought varies according to the formula

$D = 3\cos(0{\cdot}2t) + 4$

where D is the depth of water in metres at noon and t is the number of days since the drought began.

a Find the water level at the start of the drought.
b What is the water level at noon on day 6?
c What is the rate of change at noon on day 10?

contd

THE DERIVATIVE AS THE RATE OF CHANGE   contd

a $D = 3 \cos (0) + 4 = 7$ metres

b $D = 3 \cos (0.2 \times 6) + 4 = 5.1$ metres

c $D'(t) = -3 \sin (0.2t) \times 0.2 = -0.6 \sin (0.2t)$

$D'(10) = -0.6 \sin (2) = -0.5$ metres approx.

(This means that, at noon on day 10, the water level is falling at a rate of half a metre per day, although it won't *actually* fall by half a metre that day because the rate is constantly changing.)

SPEED, DISTANCE, TIME – AND ACCELERATION

Distance (or displacement), speed (velocity) and acceleration are all functions of time.

In line with Physics, the symbol used for distance is **s**

Speed (velocity) is represented by the symbol **v** and is the rate of change of distance, **s**, with time, i.e. $v = \frac{ds}{dt}$

Acceleration is the rate of change of velocity with time: $a = \frac{dv}{dt}$

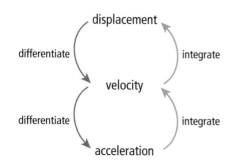

DON'T FORGET

Speed and velocity don't mean exactly the same thing, as you may know (certainly should know if you study Physics!) – but, for Higher Maths, knowing the difference isn't necessary.

Example 36

The distance travelled in metres on a roller-coaster is given by the formula

$s = 4t + 8t^2$ (*t* is the time in seconds from the start of the ride).

How fast is a car on the roller-coaster travelling at 6 seconds after setting off?

The speed, *v*, is given by $\frac{ds}{dt}$

$\frac{ds}{dt} = 4 + 16t$ and when $t = 6$, $\frac{ds}{dt} = 4 + 96 = \mathbf{100\,m/s}$

Example 37

A projectile travels at a speed *v* m/s where $v = 12t - t^2$. What distance is travelled by the projectile in the first 10 seconds after launch?

$v = \frac{ds}{dt}$ and so $s = \int v\, dt = \int (12t - t^2)\, dt = 6t^2 - \frac{1}{3}t^3 + C$

The projectile had travelled zero distance at time zero, so (0, 0) must fit the equation. Hence $C = 0$

distance $= 6t^2 - \frac{1}{3}t^3 = 6 \times 100 - \frac{1000}{3} = \mathbf{267\,m}$

DON'T FORGET

The constant of integration must be considered. It is quite often zero, but not always!

LET'S THINK ABOUT THIS

Plot the graph of the reservoir water level in the example on a graphic calculator, if you have one. Read off from the graph when the water level stops falling.

CALCULUS

MATHEMATICAL MODELLING AND OPTIMISATION

OPTIMISATION

Optimisation is finding the best/biggest/highest/loudest of various options – or maybe the lowest/cheapest/smallest option. On a graph, that would mean investigating the turning points, as was done a few pages ago. In many situations, a graph isn't really relevant or necessary, but the algebra is no different.

Maximum and minimum values of a function f(x) occur when f'(x) = 0, or at a boundary of a closed interval (see p. 63).

A table of signs will be useful to record whether f'(x) is positive or negative before and after.

Example 38

The number of tickets, T, sold for performances of an Edinburgh Festival Fringe show is related to the number of flyers, n hundred, distributed beforehand by the formula

$T = 12n^3 - n^4$

What number of flyers gives the largest number of tickets sold, and how many tickets is that?

Maximum and minimum values occur when the derivative is zero, so find $\frac{dT}{dn}$ and solve $\frac{dT}{dn} = 0$.

$\frac{dT}{dn} = 36n^2 - 4n^3 = 0$

$4n^2(9 - n) = 0$

$n = 0, n = 9$

It seems obvious that n will be 9, giving 900 flyers distributed, rather than 0, for the solution, but this must be confirmed by calculation. Evaluate $\frac{dT}{dn}$ on either side of 9.

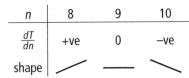

n	8	9	10
$\frac{dT}{dn}$	+ve	0	–ve
shape	/	—	\

working for nature table:

$n = 8 \Rightarrow \frac{dT}{dn} = 4 \times 64 \times 1 > 0$

$n = 10 \Rightarrow \frac{dT}{dn} = 4 \times 100 \times -1 < 0$

So, when $n = 9$, T is a **maximum**.

when $n = 9$, T $= 12 \times 9^3 - 9^4 = 2187$

A maximum of **2187 tickets** would be sold when **900 flyers** were distributed.

MATHEMATICAL MODELLING

Finding a model to help work out the optimum number of flyers can be useful in some situations. In exam questions on optimisation, you are frequently asked to set up the model in the first part of the question, then asked to maximise or minimise in the second. You will usually be asked to set up a formula for a geometric problem, with a good diagram provided.

Example 39

A rectangular plot of land is to be fenced off against a straight wall using 12 metres of fencing.

a Find an expression for the area of the plot (*i.e. set up a mathematical model*).

b Find the dimensions of the largest rectangle which can be fenced off (*this is the optimisation*).

contd

> **DON'T FORGET**
>
> You must state that the derivative is zero for maximum and minimum values.

> **DON'T FORGET**
>
> Marks will be lost if the nature of the stationary value is not checked with a nature table as shown – or using second derivative if you prefer.

> **DON'T FORGET**
>
> In the exam, if a method is not specified, you can use any valid method.

MATHEMATICAL MODELLING   contd

a Side parallel to the wall will measure $12 - 2x$ metres
Area of rectangle $= x(12 - 2x) = 12x - 2x^2$

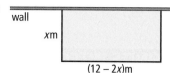

b $\frac{dA}{dx} = 12 - 4x = 0$ for maximum/minimum area

Hence $x = 3$

So, a rectangle with dimensions 3 m and 6 m will give the largest area.

Example 40

A window is to be made in the shape of a rectangle with a semicircular section above, and for structural reasons must have a perimeter of 8 metres.

a Find an expression for h in terms of x.

b Show that the area of glass is given by the formula $A = 8x - 2x^2 - \frac{1}{2}\pi x^2$

c The designer wishes to maximise the area in order to let in the maximum amount of light. Find the width of the window which will do this, to the nearest cm.

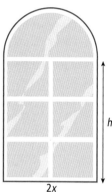

a The total length of the three straight edges and the semicircle is $2x + 2h + \pi x$

Perimeter $= 2x + 2h + \pi x = 8$
$2h = 8 - 2x - \pi x$
$h = 4 - x - \frac{\pi x}{2}$

b Area $=$ area of rectangle $+$ area of semicircle

$= 2x(4 - x - \frac{\pi x}{2}) + \frac{1}{2}\pi x^2$

$= 8x - 2x^2 - \pi x^2 + \frac{1}{2}\pi x^2$

$= 8x - 2x^2 - \frac{1}{2}\pi x^2$ (as required)

c Max/min values of the area will occur when $\frac{dA}{dx} = 0$

$\frac{dA}{dx} = 8 - 4x - \pi x = 0$

$(4 + \pi)x = 8$

$x = \frac{8}{\pi + 4} = 1 \cdot 12 \, \text{m}$

To show this is a minimum area, calculate $\frac{dA}{dx}$ for $x = 1 \cdot 10$ and $1 \cdot 15$ (for example).

x	1·10	1·12	1·15
$\frac{dA}{dx}$	0·144	0	−0·213
shape	/	—	\

Working for the nature table:

$x = 1 \cdot 10 \quad \frac{dA}{dx} = 8 - 1 \cdot 10(4 + \pi) = 0 \cdot 144$

$x = 1 \cdot 15 \quad \frac{dA}{dx} = 8 - 1 \cdot 15(4 + \pi) = -0 \cdot 213$

Hence the value of 1·12 m for x gives the maximum area for the window.

> **DON'T FORGET**
>
> In an exam, you would need to justify the nature of the stationary point. A nature table is the usual way. However, you should take a look at the "Let's Think About This" at the foot of the page (and its answer) too.

> **DON'T FORGET**
>
> The nature table is enough justification for there being a minimum at $x = 1 \cdot 12$. The working does not have to be shown.

LET'S THINK ABOUT THIS

In example 35, there is another reason you could use to justify that $x = 3$ gives a maximum area. What is it?

INTEGRATION AND AREA

DEFINITE INTEGRALS

Using F(x) to stand for the integral of f(x),

$$\int_a^b f(x)dx = F(b) - F(a)$$

Method: integrate

evaluate the result for $x = b$ and for $x = a$ (a and b are the limits)

find the difference: upper limit value minus lower limit value.

Reminder of how to set out the working:

$$\int_{-1}^{2} 5x^4\,dx = [x^5]_{-1}^{2}$$ integrate the expression

$$= 2^5 - (-1)^5$$ substitute the limit values and subtract

$$= 32 + 1 = 33$$

AREA UNDER A CURVE

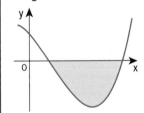

This means the area between the curve and the x-axis. Definite integrals are involved when calculating areas.

Area above the x-axis: positive value
Area below the x-axis: negative value.

Example 41

Find the area enclosed between the curve with equation $y = x^3 - 3x^2 - x + 3$ and the x-axis, as shown in the diagram.

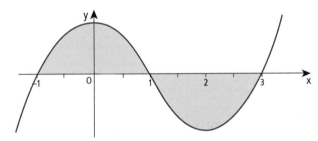

We need the points of intersection of the curve with the x-axis. Using the factorisation methods earlier in this book, we can obtain:

$y = (x - 1)(x + 1)(x - 3)$ so the intersections with the x-axis are at $-1, 1$ and 3.

Integral $A = \int_{-1}^{1}(x^3 - 3x^2 - x + 3)dx$ equation of curve, with limits at intersections

$$= \left[\frac{x^4}{4} - x^3 - \frac{x^2}{2} + 3x\right]_{-1}^{1}$$ integrating

$$= (\tfrac{1}{4} - 1 - \tfrac{1}{2} + 3) - (\tfrac{1}{4} + 1 - \tfrac{1}{2} - 3)$$ value when $x = 1$ minus value when $x = -1$

$$= 4$$ great care is needed with signs to get this right

Integral $B = \int_{1}^{3}(x^3 - 3x^2 - x + 3)dx = -4$ so area of 4 lying below the x-axis

Total area = 8 square units made up of 4 above and 4 below.

Important point for the exam:

There are usually very few marks given for the numerical evaluation at the end. Don't spend too much time on it. If you get into a tangle with fractions and negatives, cut your losses by doing other questions first and come back if you have time at the end.

AREA BETWEEN TWO CURVES

To find an area, you need

1 the formulas for both curves

2 the x-coordinates of the points where the curves intersect a and b.

$$\text{Area} = \int_a^b (f(x) - g(x))dx$$

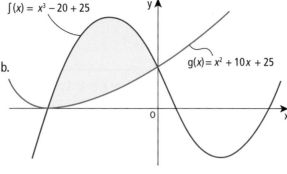

$f(x) = x^3 - 20 + 25$

$g(x) = x^2 + 10x + 25$

Example 42

Calculate area A on the graph.

Solve $x^3 - 20x + 25 = x^2 + 10x + 25$ to find intersections

$\Rightarrow x^3 - x^2 - 30x = 0 \Rightarrow x(x^2 - x - 30) = 0 \Rightarrow x(x - 6)(x + 5) = 0$

$\Rightarrow x = 0 \quad x = 6 \quad x = -5$

From the sketch in the question, we can see that −5 and 0 are the values we will need to evaluate between.

$$\text{Area} = \int_{-5}^{0} ((x^3 + 20x - 25) - (x^2 + 10x + 25))dx$$

$$= \int_{-5}^{0} (x^3 - x^2 - 30x)dx$$

$$= \left[\frac{x^4}{4} - \frac{x^3}{3} - 15x^2 \right]_{-5}^{0}$$

$$= 177 \text{ (3 sf)}$$

DON'T FORGET

It does not matter about bits above and below the x-axis for areas between two curves – it works out correctly anyway. But it does matter that we put 'f(x) − g(x)' because f(x) is above g(x) – if you reverse the order in the working above, the answer will come out with the correct magnitude but negative. Exam questions usually give a helpful diagram so you can tell which curve is above.

EVALUATING DEFINITE INTEGRALS WITH TRIG EXPRESSIONS A/B

Unit 3

Example 43

Find the area enclosed by the graph $y = \cos(2x)$, the x-axis and the lines $x = 0$ and $x = 2\pi$

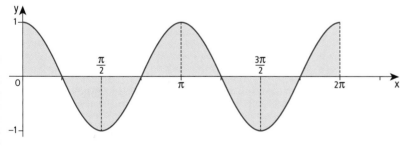

The area is partly above and partly below the x-axis. From the symmetry, we know that the areas above and below are equal. However, as the area for each section of $\frac{\pi}{4}$ radians has identical area (look at the graph), an efficient way of working would be to calculate

$$8\int_{0}^{\frac{\pi}{4}} \cos(2x)dx = 8\left[\frac{1}{2} \sin(2x) \right]_{0}^{\frac{\pi}{4}} = 4 \sin\frac{\pi}{2} - 4 \sin 0 = 4 - 0 = 4$$

LET'S THINK ABOUT THIS

Can you say why finding the area between $y = \tan x$ and the x-axis between the same limits, as in the example above, isn't possible?

BASICS – TRIANGLES, RADIANS, GRAPHS

Trigonometry can feel like a jumble of bits and pieces only connected by the words sine, cosine and tangent, rather than one subject, when you are learning it. As you reach the end of the Higher course, it's good to get an overview and see that it really is a sensible and coherent subject.

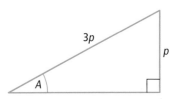

The word trigonometry comes from the words for triangle and measure. The familiar trig ratios come from measuring in triangles:

The rotating arm of length r, and the angle of rotation θ, along with the values of x and y, the horizontal and vertical components, generate values of sine, cosine and tangent for any angle:

$$\sin \theta = \frac{y}{r} \qquad \cos \theta = \frac{x}{r} \qquad \tan \theta = \frac{y}{x}$$

Using these ratios along with $x^2 + y^2 = r^2$ (Pythagoras, of course), we have what we need to solve right-angled triangles, as done in earlier Maths courses.

DON'T FORGET

These results are often remembered as SOHCAHTOA.

DON'T FORGET

Solving triangles is the work of Standard Grade, and it is expected that you are competent. You may have to use these results from time to time in Higher – and the formulas are not given in the Higher exam formula list.

Example 1

Find the size of angle A.

$$\sin A = \frac{p}{3p} = \frac{1}{3} \Rightarrow A = \sin^{-1}\frac{1}{3} = \mathbf{19{\cdot}5°}$$

The Sine Rule and the Cosine Rule can be derived, giving us the means to solve any triangle:

Sine Rule

$$\frac{a}{\sin A} = \frac{b}{\sin B} = \frac{c}{\sin C}$$

Area of triangle $= \frac{1}{2} ab \sin C$

Cosine Rule

$$a^2 = b^2 + c^2 - 2bc(\cos A)$$

$$\cos A = \frac{b^2 + c^2 - a^2}{2bc}$$

Rotating beyond the first quadrant, notice that the values of x and y are no longer necessarily positive.

If the rotating arm continues rotating, the whole cycle of lengths and ratios repeats over and over again, every 2π radians or 360°. (Radians are explained on the next page, in case you've forgotten.) If values are plotted on a graph, the three familiar trig graphs appear opposite:

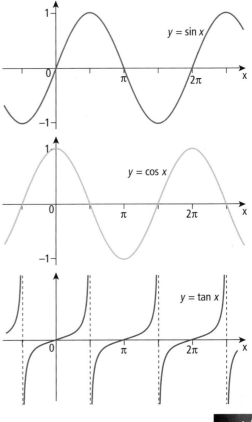

contd

contd

These graphs occur in many contexts, for example all sorts of waves – sound waves, light waves, radio waves.

Trigonometry would have been used for many practical purposes from ancient times. A knowledge of trigonometry and the stars would have helped early mariners to navigate. Sat nav uses trigonometry. Civil engineers need it to design bridges.

ANGLES

Radians are very suitable for trig calculations in the real-life uses of trig with which scientists and engineers work. A radian is the size of the angle subtending an arc the length of the circle's radius, so it needs 2π of them to make a circumference. But $360°$ is the angle in degrees to rotate round the entire circumference, so 2π radians = $360°$, or π **radians = 180°**.

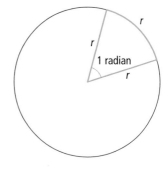

Changing from degrees to radians or vice versa can be done as shown.

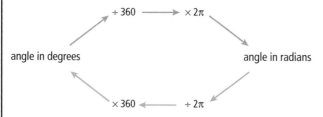

> **DON'T FORGET**
>
> Think of these two ways of measuring angles in the same sense as the two ways we use for measuring length – km and miles. In any one example, you stick to one or other – you don't mix them up. But, occasionally, you may have a reason to change from one system to the other.

However, some folk get the idea that an angle measured in radians has to have π in it. This isn't so! π is after all just a real number, 3·14159 … (or 3·14 approximately).

The equation $\sin x = 0\cdot9$ …

gives $x = \sin^{-1}(0\cdot9) = 1\cdot12$ radians as one solution – and that's fine!

So, why use π at all?

Think about the graph repeating, giving multiple solutions,

$x = 1\cdot12, 7\cdot40, 13\cdot68, 19\cdot96, …$ is a series of angles going up 6·28 or 2π at a time – but it's not exactly obvious, is it?

$x = \frac{\pi}{6}, \frac{\pi}{6} + 2\pi, \frac{\pi}{6} + 4\pi, \frac{\pi}{6} + 6\pi, …$ is preferable. It shows the pattern much better.

If you are working with radians in Paper 1, without a calculator, you will be working with fractions of π, but in Paper 2 you may be working with radians expressed as decimals.

> **DON'T FORGET**
>
> Make sure you notice whether you are to work in degrees or radians. No degree sign ° given in the trig ratios in the question, and mentions of a range for answers with π, are two big giveaways that you are expected to work in radians.

LET'S THINK ABOUT THIS

Change the angles in the list above $\frac{\pi}{6}, \frac{\pi}{6} + 2\pi, \frac{\pi}{6} + 4\pi, \frac{\pi}{6} + 6\pi$ into degrees.

PERIOD, AMPLITUDE AND TRIG EQUATIONS

PERIOD AND AMPLITUDE OF TRIG GRAPHS

DON'T FORGET

Make sure you fully understand all this, with the help of the graphs, because it is involved in many exam questions.

One wave for $y = \sin(x)$ and $y = \cos(x)$ takes 360° or 2π radians. The number of degrees or radians for one wave is called the period of the trig function. Tan (x) has a period of 180° or π radians.

Both sin (x) and cos (x) oscillate between 1 and −1. The amplitude of each is 1: they travel 1 unit above and 1 unit below their midline, the x-axis.

And the amplitude of tan (x)? Well, there is no amplitude for tan (x), because tan (x) has no maximum or minimum value.

The maximum and minimum turning points on the graphs of sine and cosine occur halfway between the zeros.

DON'T FORGET

Knowing the graphs well is helpful for finding all solutions for equations – or you can use the diagram. Notice the graph below continues in just the same way forever

EQUATIONS: SOLUTIONS WITHIN ONE WAVE 2π/360°

Looking again at the trig graphs drawn on the previous page, notice that the trig ratios never change sign – from positive to negative or vice versa – anywhere but at a multiple of $\frac{\pi}{2}$ (90°). Looking at the next diagram, showing all three trig functions on one graph, you can see that in each quadrant (90° or $\frac{\pi}{2}$ section) two of the functions are positive and one is negative. That is what gives us the helpful diagram ("all/sin/tan/cos" or CAST diagram) which we use when finding all solutions within one wave:

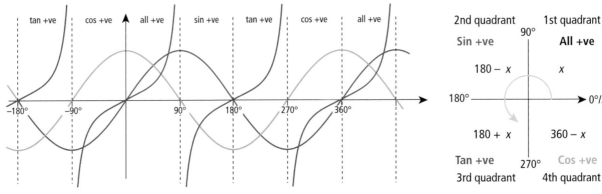

Solving a trig equation with a calculator gives one solution only. You need to find all others in the domain set for x in any particular question, or you will lose marks.

If you are inclined to make mistakes – and many candidates do, especially when negatives are involved – check the examples here carefully. No matter how complex the trig equation is, it eventually boils down to this process, so get it right.

Example 2

Solve cos $x° = -0.766$ $0 < x < 360$

Find solution from calculator for cos $x° = 0.766$
$\cos^{-1}(0.766) = 40°$

Find the other three related angles from the diagram opposite:

Select the angles which are in the quadrants where cosine is negative: 2nd and 3rd, so 140° and 220° $x = \textbf{140, 220}$

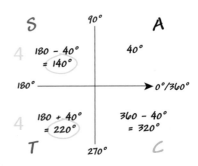

contd

EQUATIONS: SOLUTIONS WITHIN ONE WAVE 2π/360°   contd

Now, it's clear you don't actually have to *work out* all four – just the ones you need – but this work is messed up quite often, so you do need to be careful.

Of course, in Paper 2 of the exam, a graphic calculator can be used to trace the graph, which can help and reassure you; but you must still find the solutions by algebra and show your calculations to prove you used algebra.

Example 3

Solve $\tan^2 x = 4, 0 < x < 2\pi$, giving answers correct to 2 dp.

Taking the square root of both sides, $\tan x = \pm 2$

Since tangent, like all the trig functions, is positive in two quadrants and negative in two, here we want the solutions in all four quadrants, in radians:

$x = 1\cdot11$ (from calculator), **2·03, 4·25, 5·17** (from CAST diagram).

EQUATIONS: SOLUTIONS GOING BEYOND THE FIRST WAVE

From the solutions found in the first cycle of the graphs, 0°–360°, other solutions can be calculated quite easily, because the graphs repeat quite predictably.

Example 4

Solve $\tan a° = 3\cdot5 \ 0 < a < 1080$

$\tan^{-1} 3\cdot5 = 74°$ from calculator

Also, $\tan^{-1} 3\cdot5 = (180 + 74)° = 254°$

From the graph, it's easy to see that we can find more solutions by adding 360° to each of these as many times as needed to reach 1080°:

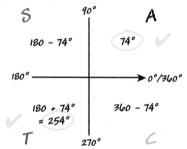

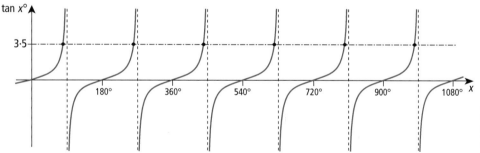

So, 74 + 360 = 434 …
74 + 2 × 360 = 794 …
74 + 3 × 360 = 1154 (over the limit!)

Similarly, 254 + 360 and 254 + (2 × 360) will give solutions.

Complete solution: **74°, 254°, 434°, 614°, 794°, 974°**

All these can be seen on the graph. Look for the symmetry.

Notice too that, since the tangent graph has period of 180°, all these answers could be obtained by adding multiples of 180° to 74°.

LET'S THINK ABOUT THIS

If a trig equation had solutions $x° = 40°$ and 320° in the domain 0 < x < 360, what would be the solutions for domain –360 < x < 0?

ADDITION AND DOUBLE-ANGLE FORMULAE

USING EXACT VALUES FOR TRIG RATIOS

Working out a ratio of sides in a triangle involves dividing, which very often leads to a value which has to be rounded off, and might also involve Pythagoras' Theorem, which might give a surd. For certain angles, you are expected to know and to be able to work with the ratios in their exact form. These angles are the ones you find in the triangles here.

> **DON'T FORGET**
>
> You need to know all these values, as they are not given in the exam formula list. But this shouldn't be some terrible memorising exercise – you will have worked with them over the year, so they should feel quite familiar.

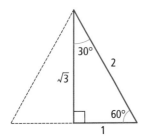

The trig ratios for these triangles, together with those for angles 0° and 90°, are summarised in this exact values table:

	0	$30°/\frac{\pi}{6}$	$45°/\frac{\pi}{4}$	$60°/\frac{\pi}{3}$	$90°/\frac{\pi}{2}$
sin	0	$\frac{1}{2}$	$\frac{1}{\sqrt{2}}$	$\frac{\sqrt{3}}{2}$	1
cos	1	$\frac{\sqrt{3}}{2}$	$\frac{1}{\sqrt{2}}$	$\frac{1}{2}$	0
tan	0	$\frac{1}{\sqrt{3}}$	1	$\sqrt{3}$	undefined

> **DON'T FORGET**
>
> You need to be competent in working with fractions and surds. This is work from Credit/Intermediate 2 level, so practise from a textbook from either of these courses if you need to sharpen up your skills.

Knowing the shape of the trig graphs will give you the ratios for 0° and 90° if you forget, and you can always draw the equilateral or isosceles triangles above to find the others if you forget.

Make sure you have spotted helpful patterns: sin 30° = cos 60°, for example.

ADDITION AND DOUBLE-ANGLE FORMULAE

You will have explored the following results, which you need to be familiar with so that you can use them confidently:

$\sin (A \pm B) = \sin A \cos B \pm \cos A \sin B$

$\cos (A \pm B) = \cos A \cos B \mp \sin A \sin B$

$\sin 2A = 2 \sin A \cos A$

$\cos 2A = \cos^2 A - \sin^2 A$
$\qquad = 2 \cos^2 A - 1$
$\qquad = 1 - 2 \sin^2 A$

this last one gives **three** possible choices for cos 2A.

> **DON'T FORGET**
>
> These are given in the formula list at the front of the exam paper.

Phew – four fewer things to remember.

Since these results are always true, regardless of the values for A and B, you can substitute the right-hand side for the left and vice versa any time it looks as if it will simplify what you are trying to do.

contd

ADDITION AND DOUBLE-ANGLE FORMULAE   contd

Example 7

In triangle AOB, show that the exact value of sin $(p + q)$ is $\frac{3}{\sqrt{10}}$

Expand: $\sin (p + q) = \sin p \cos q + \cos p \sin q$

$OB = \sqrt{2}$ and $OA = \sqrt{5}$ both by using Pythagoras' Theorem.

Using these, the four ratios in the expansion can be worked out.

When they are substituted into the addition formula, the result is:

$\sin (p + q) = \dfrac{1}{\sqrt{2}} \times \dfrac{1}{\sqrt{5}} + \dfrac{1}{\sqrt{2}} \times \dfrac{2}{\sqrt{5}}$

$\qquad\qquad = \dfrac{1}{\sqrt{10}} + \dfrac{2}{\sqrt{10}} = \dfrac{3}{\sqrt{10}}$ as required.

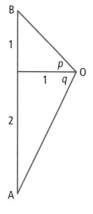

DON'T FORGET

The word "exact" means "not a rounded decimal from the calculator" as far as your Higher Maths exam is concerned, and it may include a surd.

Example 8

Find the exact values of cos a, cos $2a$ and cos $3a$, where a is the size of angle A in the diagram.

First, calculate the hypotenuse and write down cos a:

$AC = \sqrt{17}$

$\cos a = \dfrac{4}{\sqrt{17}}$

Next, use the double-angle formula for cos $2a$:

$\cos 2a = 2\cos^2 a - 1$

$\qquad = 2 \times \dfrac{16}{17} - 1$

$\qquad = \dfrac{15}{17}$ (other versions of the formula could be used)

We obtain cos $3a$ by writing it as $\cos (2a + a) = \cos 2a \cos a - \sin 2a \sin a$

We will have to calculate the value of sin a and sin $2a$ before substituting, going back to the original triangle.

$\sin a = \dfrac{1}{\sqrt{17}}$

$\sin 2a = 2 \sin a \cos a$

$= 2 \times \dfrac{1}{\sqrt{17}} \times \dfrac{4}{\sqrt{17}} = \dfrac{8}{17}$

Finally, substituting into the cos $3a$ formula:

$\cos 3a = \cos 2a \cos a - \sin 2a \sin a$

$\qquad = \dfrac{15}{17} \times \dfrac{4}{\sqrt{17}} - \dfrac{8}{17} \times \dfrac{1}{\sqrt{17}}$

$\qquad = \dfrac{52}{17\sqrt{17}}$

$\qquad = \dfrac{52\sqrt{17}}{289}$

DON'T FORGET

Should you be asked to leave an answer with a rational denominator, don't forget to check you haven't left a surd there.

LET'S THINK ABOUT THIS

Show that sin $(p + q) = \frac{3}{\sqrt{10}}$ (from the example earlier) by a different method, not involving an "addition formula" method. Hint – you can easily find all the sides in triangle ABO.

SOLVING EQUATIONS USING DOUBLE-ANGLE FORMULAE

FINDING ALL SOLUTIONS WHERE THE PERIOD IS NOT 360°

A change of period affects the finding of solutions to trig equations – there will no longer necessarily be two solutions in each 2π or 360°.

Example 11

Solve $\cos 2x° = 0.11$ $0 < x < 360$, giving x correct to 1 dp.

The simplest way to find the solutions is to find all the solutions for 2x up to 720, then halve all the answers to find x. These will cover the range 0 to 360.

$\cos^{-1} 0.11 = 83.68°$	from calculator
$2x = 83.68, 276.32$	from all/sin/tan/cos diagram
also $2x = (83.68 + 360), (276.32 + 360)$	repetitions in next cycle on graph
$2x = 83.68, 276.32, 443.68, 636.32$	all solutions for 2x in range
$x = 41.8, 138.2, 221.8, 318.2$	rounding off to 1 dp.

The graph shows you that these fit – you could draw the graph on a graphic calculator to check.

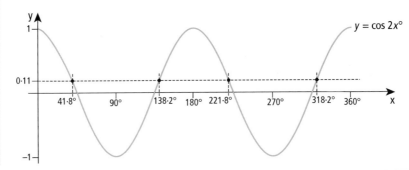

SOLVING EQUATIONS USING DOUBLE-ANGLE FORMULAE A/B

The key thing to notice is that equations on this topic will include angles like "x" and "2x" in the one equation. You must make all the angles the same (x, generally) to solve the equation, and this is the first thing to deal with.

"sin 2x" or "cos 2x" needs to be rewritten using one of the double-angle formulae in the exam formula list. No problem for sin 2x, but there is a choice for cos 2x. Choose so that the equation will end up with only sin, or only cos.

Example 12

$$\cos 2x° + 3 \sin x° - 2 = 0 \qquad 0 \le x \le 360$$
$$(1 - 2 \sin^2 x)° + 3 \sin x° - 2 = 0 \qquad \text{substituting sin version of cos 2x formula}$$
$$-2 \sin^2 x° + 3 \sin x° - 1 = 0$$
$$2 \sin^2 x° - 3 \sin x° + 1 = 0$$
$$(2 \sin x° - 1)(\sin x° - 1) = 0$$
$$2 \sin x° = 1 \text{ or } \sin x° = 1$$
$$\sin x = \tfrac{1}{2} \text{ or } \sin x° = 1$$
$$x = 30, 180 - 30, x = 90$$

so the solution is $x = 30, 90, 150$.

contd

SOLVING EQUATIONS USING DOUBLE-ANGLE FORMULAE contd

Now, this work isn't done very well in exams, and part of the problem is that it looks very complicated when you have factorising quadratic equations with trigonometry in them. So, a good way to write it from the second line onwards is:

Let s stand for sin $x°$ $(1 - 2s^2) + 3s - 2 = 0$

$$-2s^2 + 3s - 1 = 0 \qquad \text{collect terms}$$
$$2s^2 - 3s + 1 = 0 \qquad \text{make leading term +ve}$$
$$(2s - 1)(s - 1) = 0 \qquad \text{factorise quadratic}$$
$$2s = 1 \quad s = 1 \qquad \text{and then go back to writing sin } x$$
$$2 \sin x = 1 \quad \sin x = 1 \qquad \text{as before.}$$

It's up to you to decide whether you feel you would benefit from writing the equation like this.

> **DON'T FORGET**
>
> This way makes it easier to see as a straightforward quadratic equation without being put off by the trig.

Example 13

Solve $3 \cos 4x - 2 = \cos 2x$ $0 \le x \le \pi$

$4x$ is twice $2x$, so make the substitution $\cos 4x = 2 \cos^2 2x - 1$

The equation becomes: $3 (2 \cos^2 2x - 1) - 2 = \cos 2x$

Let $c = \cos 2x$: $3 (2C^2 - 1) - 2 = C$
$$6C^2 - C - 5 = 0$$
$$(6C + 5)(C - 1) = 0$$
$$6C = -5$$
$$C = 1$$

$\cos 2x = -\frac{5}{6}$ or $\cos 2x = 1$

$2x = \cos^{-1}\left(\frac{5}{6}\right) = \pi + 0 \cdot 59, \ \pi - 0 \cdot 59$ $2x = 0, 2\pi$

$x = 1 \cdot 28, 1 \cdot 87$ $x = 0, \pi$

Arrange solutions in order: **$x = 0, 1 \cdot 28, 1 \cdot 87, 3 \cdot 14$**

> **DON'T FORGET**
>
> You're in trouble if you forget that c stands for cos **$2x$**, not cos x.

> **DON'T FORGET**
>
> To get all values for x up to π, we need values for $2x$ up to 2π.

Example 14

Solve $3 \sin 2x° + 5 \cos x = 0$ $0 < x < 360$

The only substitution possible is $\sin 2x = 2 \sin x \cos x$

So, equation becomes: $6 \sin x° \cos x° + 5 \cos x° = 0$

Use s and c this time: $6sc + 5c = 0$

"c" is a common factor: $c(6s + 5) = 0$

$c = 0$ $6s + 5 = 0$

$\cos x = 0$ $6 \sin x = -5$

$x = 90$ $\sin x = -\frac{5}{6}$

               $x = 180 + 56 \cdot 4, \ 360 - 56 \cdot 4$

Solution: 90, 236·4, 270, 303·6

LET'S THINK ABOUT THIS

If an equation involving the angle $\frac{x°}{3}$ is to be solved for $0 \le x \le 720$, what range of angles would we work within to solve for $\frac{x}{3}$?

TRANSFORMATIONS OF TRIG GRAPHS

CHANGING THE AMPLITUDE: $y = a \sin x$

The work here is no different from the graph transformations revised elsewhere in this book. "a" will stretch (or compress for $-1 < a < 1$) the graph vertically. The amplitude will be a. (Amplitude can't be negative – just ignore the negative sign if $a < 0$.)

If a is negative, the graph is also reflected in the x-axis.

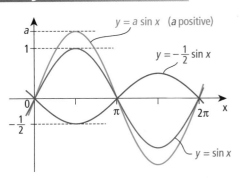

VERTICAL SHIFTS: $y = (\sin x) + a$

$y = \cos x - 2$ is the graph of $y = \cos x$ moved 2 units down (as shown opposite).

To draw the graph of $y = \frac{1}{2} - 2 \cos x$ involves more than one transformation. First, rewrite it as $y = -2 \cos (x) + \frac{1}{2}$, as this makes it easier to see what has been done to cos x. Working outwards from x, the first to consider is the result of "-2", which is to double the amplitude and reflect the graph in the x-axis. Then "$+ \frac{1}{2}$" moves the resulting graph up $\frac{1}{2}$ as shown below

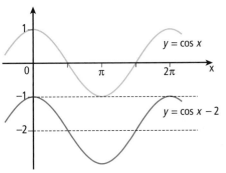

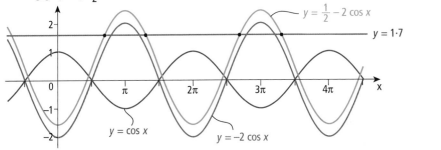

SOLVING EQUATIONS BASED ON THE ABOVE TRANSFORMATIONS

Example 5

Solve $\frac{1}{2} - 2\cos x = 1·7$ $0 < x < 4\pi$

Notice the line $y = 1·7$ drawn on the graph above.

Rearrange: $-2 \cos x = 1·2$
$$\cos x = -0·6$$
$$x = \cos^{-1} -0·6$$

First, $\cos^{-1} 0·6 = 0·93$ rads (from calculator).

Find two solutions, in the correct quadrants: $x = 2·21, 4·07$

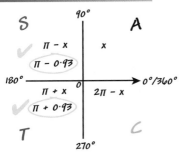

contd

SOLVING EQUATIONS BASED ON THE ABOVE TRANSFORMATIONS   contd

Add 2π to each to find the repetitions in the next cycle of the graph:

$2\cdot21 + 2\pi = 8\cdot49$, $4\cdot07 + 2\pi = 10\cdot35$

Full solution: $x = 2\cdot21, 4\cdot07, 8\cdot49, 10\cdot35$

The graph confirms (approximately) these results.

TRANSFORMATIONS: CHANGING THE WAVELENGTH/ PERIOD – $y = \sin(ax)$, $a > 0$

The graph of $\sin(ax)$ has "a" waves fitted in along the horizontal axis where normally one would be. The period of $y = \sin x$ is 2π, but for $\sin(ax)$ is $\frac{2\pi}{a}$. Exactly the same applies to $\cos(ax)$.

Here is the graph of $y = \tan 3x°$, $0 \le x \le 180$. The graph is squashed so that three times as much is fitted into 360°.

As $\tan x$ has a period of 180°, there will now be three cycles in 180°, as shown.

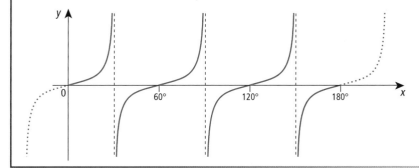

HORIZONTAL SHIFTS: GRAPH OF $y = \sin(x - a)$, AND $\cos(x - a)$, $a > 0$

Again, from what was found when doing non-trig graph transformations, this is a shift to the right of a radians.

Example 6

The graph shown has equation
$y = \cos(x - a)$

Find a.

The graph of $y = \cos x$ passes through (0, 1). The graph shown

passes through $\left(\frac{3\pi}{4}, 1\right)$ so is a shift

to the right of $\frac{3\pi}{4}$. $y = \cos\left(x - \frac{3\pi}{4}\right)$ so $a = \frac{3\pi}{4}$.

DON'T FORGET

A graphic calculator is immensely useful for checking this work. To confirm this example with a graphic calculator, graph $y = \frac{1}{2} - \cos 2x$ and $y = 1\cdot7$ on the same graph. Set an appropriate window – include at least from 0 to 4π and choose something suitable for y min and max – it can be easily adapted if you misjudge and the graph doesn't fit. You can then check the points of intersection of the two graphs, which is where the y-coordinates are the same, making $\frac{1}{2} - \cos 2x$ equal to 1·7.

DON'T FORGET

Right/left shifts don't go with our natural instincts – remember plus goes left and subtract goes right.

LET'S THINK ABOUT THIS

Can you express the equation of the graph shown in two ways, one involving sine and one cosine?

Can you go further and express it in two ways for each, for example, as $\sin(x + ...)$ and as $\sin(x - ...)$?

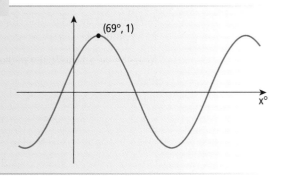
(69°, 1)

MORE GRAPH TRANSFORMATIONS AND THREE-DIMENSIONAL GEOMETRY

IDENTIFYING GRAPHS USING COMBINATIONS OF TRANSFORMATIONS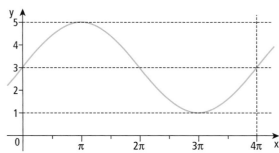

This crops up quite often in the exam. It is more likely that you will be given a graph and asked to write down its equation, than given an equation and asked to draw the graph. However, if you **are** asked to draw a graph, remember that what the examiner wants to see is that you know the basic shape, where it cuts the axes, and what its amplitude is. There are no marks for artistic impression!

DON'T FORGET

It helps to identify the transformations from the inside (close to x) out. To sketch a graph, reverse the order.

Example 9

The graph with equation
$y = a \sin(bx) + c$ is shown. Write down the values of a, b and c.

So, start with b. The normal period is 2π, but this graph takes 4π for one cycle, so half a wave fits into 2π. This means $b = \frac{1}{2}$.

The graph goes up and down between 1 and 5, so the amplitude is 2 (it goes 2 above and 2 below its midline). $a = 2$

Finally, since the midline of the graph is $y = 3$, the graph has been moved 3 units up, so $c = 3$. Its equation is $y = 2 \sin\left(\frac{1}{2}x\right) + 3$

Example 10

The diagram shows a sketch of part of a trig graph whose equation is of the form
$y = p \cos(qx°) + r$

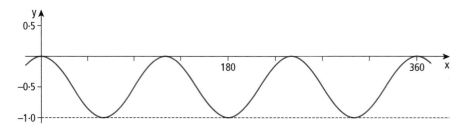

DON'T FORGET

Remember that the amplitude is half of the distance between highest and lowest values of y.

Determine the values of p, q and r.

Starting from the graph $y = \cos x$, we see what transformations are needed to change it into the graph in the diagram. Looking at the period of the graph, we see that one wave takes 120°, so three fit the normal 360°. $q = 3$

Next, look at the amplitude. The wave fits between the lines $y = -1$ and $y = 0$ (the x-axis), so its amplitude is $\frac{1}{2}$. $p = \frac{1}{2}$

Now, the vertical shift. The midline is the line $y = \frac{1}{2}$, so the graph has been moved **down** $\frac{1}{2}$. So, $r = -\frac{1}{2}$.

The graph has equation $y = \frac{1}{2}\cos(3x) - \frac{1}{2}$

Solution: $p = \frac{1}{2}$, $q = 3$, $r = -\frac{1}{2}$

ANGLES AND PLANES

This is a topic in the course (seldom tested – but maybe they're working out right now how to get it into this year's exam!) which could crop up in any question with a three-dimensional diagram. It is the identification of the angle between a line and a plane, and between two planes.

Angle between the line PY and the plane WXZ in the regular tetrahedron

The projection of the line PY on the plane WXZ is the line AY (this can be thought of as the shadow of PY on the plane if light were shining down onto the plane at right angles to the plane).

The vertex of the angle between the line and the plane is the point where they intersect: Y. The angle is $A\hat{Y}P$ (or $X\hat{Y}P$).

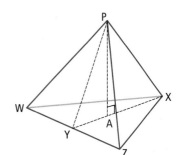

Angle between the two planes, PSVU and QUVR

Find the line of intersection of the two planes. This will be a line on which all of the points are on both planes. Here, it is UV.

Take a line in each plane perpendicular to the line of intersection, which meet at a point on it. Here, PU and QU are each perpendicular to UV and meet at U.

The angle made by these lines is the angle between the planes: $P\hat{U}Q$.

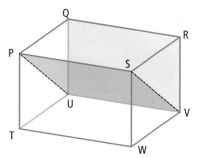

Example 10

ABCD is a rectangular plot of ground and PB is a vertical pole. Ropes connect P to the corners A, C and D.

Calculate **a** the angle between the line PD and the plane ABCD.

Calculate **b** the angle between the planes PCD and ABCD.

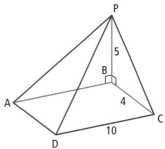

a   Line and plane meet at D. The projection of PD on the plane is BD. The angle required is PDB. B is a right angle.

$$BD = \sqrt{10^2 + 4^2} = \sqrt{116} \qquad \tan P\hat{D}B = \frac{5}{\sqrt{116}}$$
$$P\hat{D}B = 24\cdot9°$$

b   The planes intersect along line CD. PC and BC are each perpendicular to CD, meeting at C, so the required angle is $P\hat{C}B$.

In right-angled triangle PCB, $\tan P\hat{C}B = \frac{5}{4}$
$$P\hat{C}B = 51\cdot3°$$

LET'S THINK ABOUT THIS

To draw the graph of $y = -2 \sin x + 1$, the effect of the values −2, and 1 must be considered. In what order should you deal with them?

WAVE FUNCTION: $k \cos (x - \alpha)$

EXPRESSING a sin x + b cos x AS A SINGLE TRIGONOMETRIC IDENTITY

When waves are added together, they produce new waves, which you can watch happening down by the beach – although it's not just with waves in water that it happens. This topic works out what the equations for some of these new waves will be.

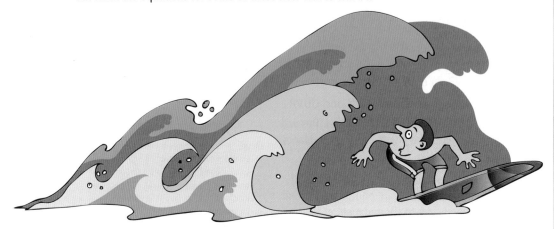

The waves you add will be a sine and a cosine with the same period (i.e. they will both be functions of the same variable, x, or $2x$, or $\frac{1}{2}x$).

The new combined wave has the same period but with a phase shift (moved along a bit – that's the "α" in $k \cos (x - \alpha)$).

The new wave also has an altered amplitude "k" in $k \cos (x - \alpha)$.

WORKING WITH OTHER VERSIONS OF THE WAVE FORMULA

If you look at the "Let's think about this" on p. 79, and the answer, you can remind yourself that a sine/cosine wave can be expressed in (at least) four different ways. In this work, you could be asked to express your answer as $k \cos (x - \alpha)$ $k \sin (x - \alpha)$
$k \cos (x + \alpha)$ or $k \sin (x + \alpha)$.

Here we go with quite a difficult example – but with lots of explanations to remind you of all the steps you might have to do.

Example 15

Express $4 \cos x° - 3 \sin x°$ in the form $k \sin (x + \alpha)°$, where $0 \le x \le 360$ and $k > 0$.

Use an addition formula to expand $\sin (x + \alpha)°$:

$\sin (x + \alpha) = \sin x \cos \alpha + \cos x \sin \alpha$

So, equating the two expressions, and multiplying the right-hand side through by k:

$4 \cos x° - 3 \sin x° = k \sin x° \cos °\alpha + k \cos x° \sin \alpha°$

In red are two terms in cos x, which must be equal, and two in blue for sine:

$k \cos x° \sin \alpha° = 4 \cos x° \quad\quad \Rightarrow k \sin \alpha = 4 \Rightarrow k^2 \sin^2 \alpha = 16$

$k \sin x° \cos°\alpha = -3 \sin x° \quad\quad \Rightarrow k \cos \alpha = -3 \Rightarrow k^2 \cos^2 \alpha = 9$

Adding the left and right sides of the two equations together:

$k^2 \sin^2 \alpha + k^2 \cos^2 \alpha = 16 + 9 \Rightarrow k^2 = 25 \Rightarrow k = 5$

contd

DON'T FORGET

In the exam, the question will most likely specify which form you have to use. It will probably be the one that works out easiest, with positive signs keeping α in the first quadrant, but the method is the same way anyway. You will be given a range for α, such as $0 \le x \le 90$, but you can expect to get the answer in the correct range without having to alter anything.

DON'T FORGET

The addition formulae are in the list at the front of the exam paper and on p.74 in this book.

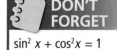

WORKING WITH OTHER VERSIONS OF THE WAVE FORMULA   contd

Also $\frac{k \sin \alpha}{k \cos \alpha} = -\frac{4}{3} \Rightarrow \tan \alpha° = -\frac{4}{3}$

We need the angle α to be in the correct quadrant to make sin +ve, cos –ve and tan –ve to match values found in the working above – and that means 2nd quadrant.

$\alpha = 180 - 53 \cdot 1 = 126 \cdot 9$

Answer: $4 \cos x° - 3 \sin x° = \mathbf{5 \sin (x + 126 \cdot 9)°}$

The next examples have been done with all the working you should be writing down but without so much explanation of what is being done.

Here is an example which could be in Paper 1, with no calculator allowed (so using exact values), and with angles in radians:

Example 16

Express $\cos \theta + \sqrt{3} \sin \theta$ in the form $k \cos (\theta - \alpha)$, $0 \le \alpha \le \frac{\pi}{2}$, $k > 0$.

$\cos \theta + \sqrt{3} \sin \theta = k \cos (\theta - \alpha)$
$\qquad\qquad = k \cos \theta \cos \alpha + k \sin \theta \sin \alpha$

$k \cos \alpha = 1$ and $k \sin \alpha = \sqrt{3}$

$k^2 = 1^2 + (\sqrt{3})^2 = 1 + 3 = 4$

$k = 2$

$\tan \alpha = \sqrt{3}$

$\qquad \alpha = \frac{\pi}{3}$ (1st-quadrant answer, since sin, cos and tan are all positive)

$\cos \theta + \sqrt{3} \sin \theta = \mathbf{2 \cos (\theta - \frac{\pi}{3})}$

In modelling examples from the real world, the angles may be multiples of $x°$ or, in this next example, $t°$. We will come back to this example in the next section and develop it further, but for now:

Example 17

The formula $d(t) = 250(\cos 30t° - \sin 30t°) + 450$ gives the approximate depth of the water in a harbour t hours after midnight.

Express $(\cos 30t° - \sin 30t°)$ in the form $k \cos (30t - \alpha)°$, $0 \le \alpha \le 360$, $k > 0$.

$(\cos 30t° - \sin 30t°) = k \cos 30t° \cos° \alpha + k \sin 30t° \sin \alpha°$

Equating coefficients of $\cos 30t°$ and $\sin 30t°$,

$k \cos \alpha° = 1 \qquad \Rightarrow k^2 \cos^2 \alpha = 1$
$k \sin \alpha° = -1 \qquad \Rightarrow k^2 \sin^2 \alpha = 1$

$k^2 = 2 \Rightarrow k = \sqrt{2}$

$\tan \alpha° = -1 \quad \alpha = 360 - 45 = 315$ sin –ve, cos +ve, tan –ve 360 – 45 (CAST)

$(\cos 30t° - \sin 30t°) = \mathbf{\sqrt{2} \cos (30t - 315)°}$

This example will be developed further on p 86.

DON'T FORGET

$\sin^2 x + \cos^2 x = 1$

DON'T FORGET

In example 17:
sin –ve,
cos +ve,
tan –ve
so (360 – …) for answer.

 ## LET'S THINK ABOUT THIS

If $\sin \alpha < 0$, $\cos \alpha < 0$, and $\tan \alpha > 0$, what subset of the range 0 to 360 must α fall into?

USING THE WAVE FUNCTION TO SKETCH GRAPHS **Unit 3**

WAVE FORMULA AND INTERPRETING GRAPHS

Wave-formula questions in the exam are sometimes in two parts. These questions can be challenging. Many wave-formula questions involve interpreting or drawing graphs.

Example 18

a Graph 1 shows $f(x) = a \sin x°$
   What is the value of a?

Graph 2 shows $g(x) = b \cos x°$
What is the value of b?

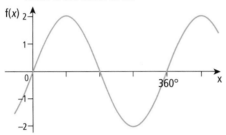

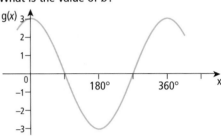

b Write $f(x) + g(x)$ in the form $k \sin (x + \alpha)°$ where $0 \le \alpha \le 90$

Solution:

a The amplitude of the first graph is 2, so $f(x) = 2 \sin x°$ $a = 2$
For the second graph, the amplitude is 3, so $g(x) = 3 \cos x°$ $b = 3$

b $f(x) + g(x) = 2 \sin x° + 3 \cos x° = k \sin (x + \alpha)°$

$2 \sin x° + 3 \cos x° = k \sin x° \cos \alpha° + k \cos x° \sin \alpha°$

$k \cos \alpha° = 2$ and $k \sin \alpha° = 3$

$k^2 = 4 + 9 = 13 \Rightarrow k = \sqrt{13}$

$\dfrac{k \sin \alpha}{k \cos \alpha} = \dfrac{3}{2}$

$\tan \alpha° = 1·5 \Rightarrow \alpha = 56·3$

$2 \sin x° + 3 \cos x° = \sqrt{13} \sin (x + 56·3)°$

SKETCH GRAPHS OF THE FORM $y = k \cos (x - \alpha) + b$

We know what the graphs of $y = 2 \sin x$ and $y = 3 \cos x$ would look like (see previous example), but this does not tell us what the graph of $y = 2 \sin x° + 3 \cos x°$ will look like.

However, once altered into its $y = \sqrt{13} \sin (x + 56·3)°$ form, we can see we have the graph of $y = \sin x$ with the amplitude altered and a horizontal shift. Now we can sketch it.

The amplitude is $\sqrt{13}$, or 3·6 approximately.

The period is 360°.

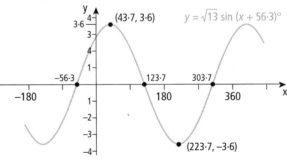

"+56·3°" tells us that the graph of $\sin x°$, which normally passes through $(0, 0)$, is moved 56·3° to the left, so the graph passes through $(-56·3, 0)$.

Sometimes, after $a \sin x + b \sin x$ has been expressed as $k \cos (x - \alpha)$, the question asks for a sketch of a related curve as in the next example.

contd

SKETCH GRAPHS OF THE FORM $y = k \cos(x - \alpha) + b$ contd

This example is hard! It has been chosen to see if you can be careful with signs and can draw quite a complex trig function:

Example 19

a Express $\cos x - \sqrt{3} \sin x$ in the form $k \sin(x - \alpha)$, $k > 0$, $0 \le \alpha \le 2\pi$

b Hence or otherwise, sketch the curve with equation
$y = 3 + \cos x - \sqrt{3} \sin x$ in the interval $0 \le x \le 2\pi$

a $\cos x - \sqrt{3} \sin x = k \sin x \cos \alpha - k \cos x \sin \alpha$

$-k \sin \alpha = 1$ $k \cos \alpha = -\sqrt{3}$

$k^2 = 1 + 3 = 4 \Rightarrow k = 2$

$\tan \alpha = \dfrac{1}{\sqrt{3}}$ 3rd quadrant: $\sin \alpha$ and $\cos \alpha$ both negative, $\tan \alpha$ positive.

$\Rightarrow \alpha = \pi + \dfrac{\pi}{6} = \dfrac{7\pi}{6}$

$\cos x - \sqrt{3} \sin x = 2 \sin\left(x - \dfrac{7\pi}{6}\right)$

Notice the question uses exact values. Such a question could be in Paper 1.

b $y = 3 + (\cos x - \sqrt{3} \sin x) = 2 \sin\left(x - \dfrac{7\pi}{6}\right) + 3$

Part **a** has allowed us to rewrite the trigonometric expression in a form which allows us to interpret the graph as a transformation of $y = \sin x$.

$\sin x$ is first moved $\dfrac{7\pi}{6}$ to the right.

The resulting graph has the amplitude increased from 1 to 2.

Finally, the graph is moved up 3.

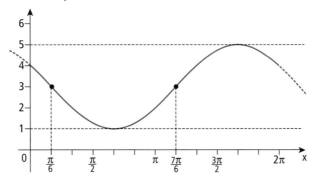

> ### DON'T FORGET
> "Hence or otherwise" you should take to mean "we strongly recommend you do this by using the result we asked you to find in the first part, but if you really want to, you can do it some other way"!

> ### DON'T FORGET
> The graph must cover the whole of the required range of values for x: in this case, $0 \le x \le 2\pi$.

SKETCHING TRIG GRAPHS IN GENERAL A/B

All the graphs you will be asked to draw or interpret will be based on the types of transformations explored in this chapter.

Here is a graph showing all these transformations applied to $y = \sin x°$:

You are not likely to have all these features in any one question, however!

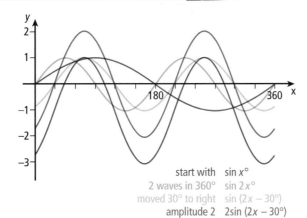

start with $\sin x°$
2 waves in 360° $\sin 2x°$
moved 30° to right $\sin(2x - 30°)$
amplitude 2 $2\sin(2x - 30°)$
moved down 1 $2\sin(2x - 30°) - 1$

⚙ LET'S THINK ABOUT THIS

What happens if you reflect sine/cosine graphs in the axes.

USING THE WAVE FUNCTION TO SOLVE EQUATIONS Unit 3

FINDING MAXIMUM/MINIMUM VALUES USING $k \cos (x - \alpha)$

DON'T FORGET

Any "real life" contexts will be kept simple and any "specialist knowledge" needed will be in the question. You do not have to be an expert on tides to answer questions in the exam on tides!

Example 20

Remember example 17 about the depth of water, $d(t)$, in the harbour on p. 83.

$d(t) = 450 + 250 (\cos 30t° - \sin 30t°)$
$\qquad = 450 + 250\sqrt{2} \cos (30t - 315)°$

This gives a simplified version of what happens to the water level when the tide comes in and goes out. $d(t) = 450 + 250\sqrt{2} \cos (30t - 315)°$ can be sketched.

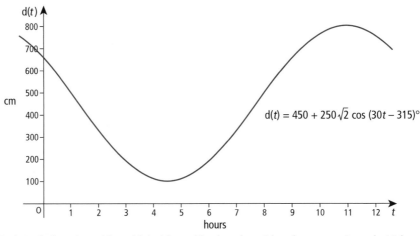

Each cycle from low tide to high tide and back to low tide takes approximately 12 hours. (In reality it takes nearer 13 hours, but that would make the maths more complicated, and we are talking "simplified version" here.) One cycle of sin/cos x takes 360°. This means 12 hours needs fitted into 360°, which is why we have "30t" in the equation. If 0 is taken as midnight, t stands for the number of hours after midnight.

DON'T FORGET

You don't actually need to know all about tides to do exam questions, but it certainly makes the topic more interesting, and possibly easier to understand if you do!

Compared to $y = \cos 30t°$, the graph has been moved 315° to the right, amplitude made $250\sqrt{2}$ times as large, and moved up 450°.

Now, it doesn't take too much thought to realise that the maximum value of $d(t)$ gives the depth of water at high tide (and minimum at low tide) and that the values of t when the maximum and minimum occur give the times of high and low tide.

We can see these values approximately on the graph.

Let's now have a part **b** to the question.

b At what time is high tide, and how high is the water level at high tide?

Solution (algebraically):

The maximum value of $\cos t°$ is 1, when $t° = 0, 360, 720$ and so on, so

$\cos (30t - 315)° = 1$
$\qquad 30t - 315 = 0, 360, 720$
$\qquad\qquad 30t = 315, 360 + 315$ and so on
$\qquad\qquad\qquad t = 10·5, ...$ (we don't need more values)

Water level $d(10·5) = 450 + 250 \times \sqrt{2} \times 1 = 803.55$

High water occurs at **10:30 am**, and the depth of water then is **804 cm**.

THE WAVE FUNCTION: SOLVING EQUATIONS

Example 21

a Express $4 \cos x - 3 \sin x$ in the form $k \cos (x + \alpha)$ where $k > 0$ and $0 \le \alpha \le \frac{\pi}{2}$

b Hence solve the equation $4 \cos x - 3 \sin x = 2$ for $0 \le x \le \frac{\pi}{2}$

Solution

a $4 \cos x - 3 \sin x = k \cos (x + \alpha)$

$\qquad \qquad = k \cos x \cos \alpha - k \sin x \sin \alpha$

$k \cos \alpha = 4, \; k \sin \alpha = 3 \Rightarrow k = 5$

$\tan \alpha = \frac{3}{4} \Rightarrow \alpha = 0 \cdot 64$

$4 \cos x - 3 \sin x = \mathbf{5 \cos (x + 0 \cdot 64)}$

b $4 \cos x - 3 \sin x = 2$

$5 \cos (x + 0 \cdot 64) = 2$

$\cos (x + 0 \cdot 64) = 0.4$

$x + 0 \cdot 64 = \cos^{-1} (0 \cdot 4) = 1 \cdot 16$

$x = 1 \cdot 16 - 0 \cdot 64 = \mathbf{0 \cdot 52}$

(This question is probably worth about seven marks in the exam.)

DON'T FORGET

"Hence" means from your work in the first part. Although trying the second part with wrong results from the first part may still get you some marks, clearly being competent in the wave formula is going to be an advantage.

DON'T FORGET

Always check to see if part (b) in a question is linked to part (a). Very often, part (a) helps you to see how to do part (b).

USING CALCULUS IN A WAVE-FORMULA QUESTION

Suppose Example 21 had this part **b** instead:

b Hence find, in the interval $0 \le x \le \pi$, the x-coordinate of the point on the curve where the gradient is –1.

You would hit problems if you tried to do this by differentiating $4 \cos x - 3 \sin x$ (by all means try it and see what happens) but changed into $k \cos (x - \alpha)$ form it can be differentiated quite easily.

$y = 5 \cos (x + 0 \cdot 64)$

$\frac{dy}{dx} = -5 \sin (x + 0 \cdot 64) = -1$

$\sin (x + 0 \cdot 64) = 0 \cdot 2$

$x + 0 \cdot 64 = 0.20, \pi - 0.20, \ldots$

$x = -0 \cdot 44, 2 \cdot 30, \ldots$

The answer in the given range is therefore $x = \mathbf{2 \cdot 30 \text{ radians}}$.

DON'T FORGET

Notice it is safely in radians, so it can be differentiated without any extra complications.

LET'S THINK ABOUT THIS

On p.86, if a vessel arriving in the early hours of the morning needs 3 m depth to sail in, what's the latest time it should arrive?

EXAM-STYLE QUESTIONS

PAPER 1 SECTION A   40 MARKS

Paper 1 is done without a calculator.
1 hour 30 minutes

First there are 20 multiple choice questions each worth 2 marks. You score 2 or 0 for each. In the exam there is no penalty for a wrong answer so it's worthwhile guessing if you really can't decide – but don't do it till the end of the exam! Mark on your question paper any ones where you can't decide between two options and make sure you leave a few moments at the end to make a last minute choice one way or the other.

(Obviously there is no advantage at all in guessing answers at any other time except the exam!)

Here are some examples, with some hints.

1. The diagram shows part of the graph of a cubic function $y = f(x)$.

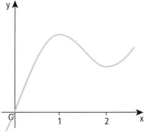

Which of the graphs below is most likely to show $y = f'(x)$?

a 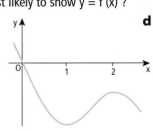   **b**   **c** 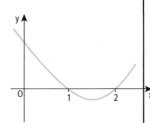   **d**

Hint – It's wise not to choose without checking all of the graphs – it's easy to find some correct features and overlook something else which is wrong. Notice the differences in the options.

2. What is the gradient of the tangent to the curve with equation $y = 3\sqrt{x}$ at the point where $x = 9$?

Hint – Best to work it out without looking at the options first.   Then if you don't see your answer, try it again.

A 9   B $\frac{1}{2}$ C 1   D $\frac{1}{6}$

3. Here are two statements about the graph with equation $y = \cos 3x°$.

(1) The graph has a minimum turning point when $x = 180$.
(2) The graph has a maximum turning point when $x = 120$.

Which one of the following is true?
A   Neither statement is correct.
B   Only statement (1) is correct.
C   Only statement (2) is correct.
D   Both statements are correct.

Hint – first sketch the graph, then examine each statement separately and decide whether it is T or F, then pick the appropriate answer from A–D.

4. The first three terms of a sequence generated by the recurrence relation $u_n = au_{n-1} + b$ are 2, 5 and 14. What are the values of a and b?

	a	b
A	3	1
B	−1	3
C	3	−1
D	1	−1

PAPER 1 SECTION B   30 MARKS

There will be a few long questions, usually in several parts. This is where you will find questions where the examiners want to test that you have essential graphical and calculation skills without relying on a calculator.

Example

(a) Express $\cos x - \sqrt{3}\sin x$ in the form $k\cos(x + \alpha)$, $k > 0$, $0 \le \alpha \le 2\pi$

(b) Hence or otherwise, sketch the curve with equation
$y = 2 + \cos x - \sqrt{3}\sin x$ in the interval $0 \le x \le 2\pi$ showing the coordinates of points where the graph meets the axes.

Notes – You must use exact values and answer in radians (though you could convert to degrees for your working). A calculator is not needed for this question. Part (b) uses the result you found in part (a) and is A/B level.

PAPER 2   60 MARKS

This doesn't mean a calculator is needed for every question, though it might be really necessary from time to time. Many questions are "calculator free" meaning they could be done with or without a calculator – you choose. Questions in several parts will tend to become harder as you go through them so don't become dispirited if you are not a strong candidate and you find you get stuck on part (c) in questions – they are probably the hard bits put there to decide who should get A grades!

| Calculator allowed |

1. The diagram shows a cuboid, and P dividing FE in the ratio 1:2

$$\overrightarrow{OA} = \begin{pmatrix} 0 \\ 0 \\ 3 \end{pmatrix} \quad \overrightarrow{OC} = \begin{pmatrix} 6 \\ 0 \\ 0 \end{pmatrix} \quad \overrightarrow{OG} = \begin{pmatrix} 0 \\ 9 \\ 0 \end{pmatrix}$$

a) Express the vector $\overrightarrow{OP}$ in component form.

b) Calculate the size of angle GOP.

c) Write down a unit vector parallel to OP.

Notes – Vectors questions don't tend to get so hard as some other questions but be careful not to make arithmetic errors – wrong numbers early on might make the working in later parts harder.

2. What is the maximum value of the function $f(x) = \frac{1}{x^2 - 6x + 11}$ $x \in R$, giving a reason for your answer?

Notes – While you might fiddle around on a calculator with this you really can't give an adequate answer without algebraic rearrangement.

3. A curve has equation $y = \cos(2x)\cos(x)$.

a) Use an appropriate trigonometric substitution to express y in terms of powers of $\cos(x)$.

b) Calculate the gradient of the tangent to the curve at the point where $x = \frac{\pi}{2}$.

Notes – (i) radians must be used throughout the question as calculus is involved;
(ii) the expression for y cannot be differentiated using only Higher work without being rewritten as asked for in part (a). Part (b) is A/B level.

Sources of exam questions are Past Higher exam papers, which can be found on the SQA website or bought in a book of Past Papers. Your maths textbook most likely has a revision section, and your teacher or lecturer has probably issued you with many revision questions.

ANSWERS TO EXAM-STYLE QUESTIONS

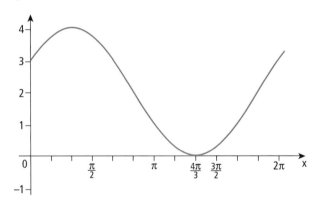

PAPER 2

1.

a) $\overrightarrow{OP} = \begin{pmatrix} 2 \\ 9 \\ 3 \end{pmatrix}$

b) Using the formulas given in the formula list for scalar product, you should arrive at

$\cos \hat{GOP} = \dfrac{81}{9\sqrt{94}}$ in your working (or the decimal equivalent) and 21.8° for the size of the angle.

c) The magnitude of $\overrightarrow{OP} = \sqrt{94}$ (obtained during the working for (b)) so the unit vector is

$\dfrac{1}{\sqrt{94}} \begin{pmatrix} 2 \\ 9 \\ 3 \end{pmatrix}$

2. Questions on restricted domains or maximum/minimum values often involve consideration of squares or roots. Here the denominator can be rewritten $(x-3)^2 + 2$ which has minimum value 2, making the maximum value of the fraction $\frac{1}{2}$. (Test other values if you're not convinced).

3.

a) The appropriate formula from the formula list on exam paper is

$\cos(2x) = 2\cos^2(x) - 1$ leading to $y = 2\cos 3(x) - \cos(x)$

b) $\dfrac{dy}{dx} = -6\cos^2 x \sin x + \sin x.$ $\sin \frac{\pi}{2} = 1$ and $\cos \frac{\pi}{2} = 0$ so the gradient is 1.

ANSWERS TO "LET'S THINK ABOUT THIS" SECTIONS

GEOMETRY

Straight line

Page 7 Vectors.

Page 9 Just by inspection, we have:
P(2, 7) (4, 3) (6, −1) Q(8, −5) (notice the pattern of x-coordinates (up 2) and y-coordinates (down 4)), giving (6, −1) as the answer. Alternatively, you could use vectors and calculate

$\frac{2q + p}{3}$ which also gives position vector $\begin{pmatrix} 6 \\ -1 \end{pmatrix}$

Page 11 In an equilateral triangle, since the three sets of lines will be exactly the same.

Circle

Page 13 You must first divide though by 4, so
$x^2 + y^2 - 4x + 2y + \frac{11}{4} = 0$

Page 15 'Elimination method' – subtract 1st equation from 2nd to obtain
$12x + 16y - 4 = 0$
or $3x + 4y - 1 = 0$

Page 17 The radius would be $\sqrt{2^2 + (-6)^2 - 50} = \sqrt{-10}$, which clearly can't exist; r must be positive for a circle to exist.

Vectors

Page 19 $\overrightarrow{AB} = \overrightarrow{AO} + \overrightarrow{OB} = -\mathbf{a} + \mathbf{b} = \mathbf{b} - \mathbf{a}$

Page 21 A sketch will show that $\overrightarrow{PS} = 2\,\overrightarrow{PQ} \Rightarrow \mathbf{s} - \mathbf{p} = 2(\mathbf{q} - \mathbf{p})$, which can be rearranged into $\mathbf{s} = 2\mathbf{q} - \mathbf{p}$. Substituting the components of $\mathbf{p}$ and $\mathbf{q}$ gives

$\mathbf{s} = \begin{pmatrix} 19 \\ -5 \\ 40 \end{pmatrix}$

Page 23 A rhombus has its diagonals perpendicular. Find the components of $\overrightarrow{AC}$ and $\overrightarrow{BD}$, then work out $\overrightarrow{AC}.\overrightarrow{BD}$. If it works out as zero, ABCD is a rhombus.

ALGEBRA

Recurrence relations

Page 25 1, 2, 3, 4, 5, … would do fine. More interesting possibilities would be 0.01, 1.01, 2.01, … or −1004.3, −1003.3, −1002.3, … . Clearly, there is an infinite number of infinite sequences which will fit the bill.

Page 27 $L = \frac{b}{1-a}$ gives a limit of −3, but the terms of the sequence 1, 5, 13, 29, 61, … don't make this look

likely. And of course it isn't, because $a = 2$, and so −1 < a < 1 isn't true – there is no limit. It does show, though, that you could walk straight into a mega-mistake by not checking.

Functions and graphs

Page 29 The graph is undefined at $x = 0$ (since $\frac{1}{0}$ is undefined). The graph increases or decreases without limit as $x = 0$ is approached from either the right or left.

Page 31 2nd quadrant: reflection in y-axis, so
$f(-x) = \frac{1}{(-x)} = -\frac{1}{x}$,
and for 4th quadrant reflection in x-axis, so
$-f(x) = -\frac{1}{x}$.
For the 3rd quadrant, either of these can be reflected in the x- or y-axis as appropriate, and we get $\frac{1}{x}$ again.

The sections in the 1st and 4th quadrants make
$f(x) = \frac{1}{x}$, $x \in R$, $x \neq 0$, and the other two sections make up $f(x) = -\frac{1}{x}$ for the same domain.

Page 33 Move $y = x^2$ 2 units to the right, stretch it vertically by a factor of 3, then move the whole thing up 5 units. (Work from x outwards in the formula to get these in the right order.)

Pages 35 and 37 Assuming the maths is correct, it shows there are no **real** roots – but, as you will discover if you do Advanced Higher, the study of square roots of negative numbers opens up a new realm of possibilities. Enjoy!

Page 39 The point of intersection of the graph with the y-axis, and the behaviour at the extremities – where x approaches $\pm \infty$

Page 41 The value of x^3 is much more significant to the value of the polynomial than either of the other terms. As x increases, $f(x)$ will increase because x^3 is large and positive, and as x decreases (x approaches $-\infty$) $f(x)$ also decreases

Exponentials and logarithms

Page 43 Any function which maps more than one value of x to one value of y. An example is $y = x^2$ where, for example, you have (2, 4) and (−2, 4). When you reverse the coordinates for the inverse, 4 is mapped to more than one image, which breaks the rules for a function.

Page 45 10 is clearly handy, as our entire number system is based on it. e on the other hand is nature's favourite number – many natural processes when analysed use e. You can investigate this on the internet after you've finished revising!

Page 47 Choose two well-separated pairs of coordinates from the table. You don't need more than two points to complete the calculations.

Page 49 Equating y –

$a^{x+1} = a^x + 1$ (remember $a^{x+1} = x^x \times a^1$)

$a \times a^x - a^x = 1$

$a^x(a - 1) = 1$

$a^x = \dfrac{1}{a-1}$

Then changing the exponential statem ent to a logarithmic one – $\log_a \dfrac{1}{a-1} = x$

CALCULUS

Page 51 $\frac{2t^3}{s}$ is a constant for the purposes of differentiating with respect to r.

The derivative $P'(r) = \frac{2t^3}{s} \times 2r = \frac{4t^3 r}{s}$

Page 53 Let $u = 5x - 2$ so that $y = \frac{3}{u^4} = 3u^{-4}\frac{dy}{du} = -12u^{-5}$

$\frac{du}{dx} = 5$ $\frac{dy}{dx} = \frac{60}{(5x-2)^5}$

Page 55 If $a = 0$, or $n = -1$, then the denominator would be zero, and division by zero is not possible.

Page 57 Let $u = \sin(x)$ so that $y = \sqrt{\sin(x)} = u^{\frac{1}{2}}$

$y = \frac{dy}{du} \times \frac{du}{dx} = \frac{1}{2}u^{-\frac{1}{2}} \times \cos(x) = \frac{\cos(x)}{2\sqrt{\sin(x)}}$

Page 59 For a polynomial function, the highest power of the derivative is one less than for the original function. The highest power of x dictates the maximum number of turning points/inflexions possible for any function, so the derived function has less potential for these.

Page 61 A "never decreasing" function can have a rising horizontal point of inflexion (see top graph on p62), but an "always increasing" one can't.

Page 63 Compare x^4 with $1\,000\,000\ x^3$. Since x can increase without limit, the first exceeds the second as soon as $x > 1\,000\,000$. It won't matter what the coefficients of lesser powers are, as the variable x can always exceed them eventually.

Page 65 Water level drops to 1 metre after 15 days. (The minimum depth of 1 metre should be no surprise in view of the constants (3 and 4) in the formula – think graph transformations.)

Page 67 As x is on the closed interval 0 to 12 (i.e. definite endpoints of 0 and 12), and both 0 and 12 would give a minimum area (0, in fact) and 3 is the only value where the derivative is 0, no other solution is possible.

Page 69 The graph of tan x is not bounded by any upper value – it increases indefinitely. So, there is no finite area to calculate.

TRIGONOMETRY

Page 71 $\frac{\pi}{6} = 30°$.

Adding 360 for 2π gives 390°, 750° and 1110°.

Page 73 −320° and −40°, obtained by subtracting 360° from each answer.

Page 75 There is an alterrnative:
Using cosine rule:

$\cos AOB = \dfrac{(\sqrt{5})^2 + (\sqrt{2})^2 + 3^2}{2 \times \sqrt{5} \times \sqrt{2}} = -\dfrac{1}{\sqrt{10}}$

$\sin^2 AOB = 1 - \cos^2 AOB = 1 - \frac{1}{10} = \frac{9}{10}$

$\Rightarrow \sin AOB = \dfrac{3}{\sqrt{10}}$

Page 77 To obtain values for x, the values for $\frac{x}{3}$ will be multiplied by 3, so we only need to solve as far as 240 for $\frac{x}{3}$. Solve from 0 to 240.

Page 79 The graph can be seen as sin x moved 21° left, or cosine moved 69° to the right. These give **$y = \sin (x + 21)°$ or $y = \cos (x - 69)°$**. Adding or subtracting multiples of 360 will not alter the graph because of periodicity, so two more possibilities are **$y = \sin (x - 339)°$ and $y = \cos (x + 291)°$**. There are more.

Page 81 Following the advice to work outwards from x, the "reflect and stretch" (−2) should be onsidered before the "vertical shift" (+1). While it often doesn't make a difference, here it does because of the reflection.

You should try stetching the graph doing the transformations in different orders and verifying the correct one using a graphic calculator.

Page 83 From CAST (or "all, sin, tan, cos") the 3rd quadrant, 180–270°.

Page 85 If a sine or cosine graph is reflected in either axis, another sine or cosine graph will be the result, so any variation can be obtained from the transformations already considered.

Page 87 Solve $450 + 250 \sqrt{2} \cos(30t - 315)° = 300$

$\cos (30t - 315)° = -\dfrac{150}{250\sqrt{2}}$

$(30t - 315)° = 115$

$30t = 430$

$t = 14.3$ (hours after midnight)

but remember that period is 12 hours.

The answer: around 2:20am.

INDEX